THE ATTORNEY'S

NETWORKING HANDBOOK

THE ATTORNEY'S NETWORKING HANDBOOK

14 Principles to Growing Your Law Practice
in Less Time with Greater Results

Second Edition

Steve Fretzin

ISBN-13: 9781548687212
ISBN-10: 1548687219

Table of Contents

Foreword by Neil Dishman

We lawyers have a disease. Steve Fretzin is the cure.

Our lawyers' disease is a severe, irrational aversion to doing business development well, or even doing it at all.

This disease has an incubation period of three years — the three years we spend in law school. There we learn little or nothing about where clients come from or how law firms make money. We are trained to think, speak, write, and act like academics, not like businesspeople. We are made to feel as if we belong to a scholarly caste that should be above common things like "sales" and "marketing."

Shortly after law school, the symptoms appear. Once in private practice, many of us avoid even trying to develop business, due to ignorance, fear, or even outright disdain of the process. And those of us who do put forth some effort are often ineffective and inefficient — which should be no surprise, given that we've had no training in it.

When it comes to networking in particular, we often waste the precious time of both ourselves and the people we're meeting. This is because we fail to be thoughtful and purposeful about selecting the people we're meeting, defining what we want accomplish with them, and agreeing on a plan to make it happen. We compound these problems by lacking discipline in our follow-up efforts.

Steve Fretzin's philosophy and techniques are a powerful antidote. I know this because I've had a heavy dose of it. I've practiced for ten years at Jackson Lewis P.C., where our business is helping employers prevent and resolve disputes with their employees. (Incidentally, it was Steve who taught me to express what I do in plain English like this, rather than saying something like "I practice management-side labor and employment law.") In 2012, just after I was elevated to become an income shareholder at my firm, I engaged Steve for a six-month course on all aspects of business development.

I had already enjoyed some success at business development up to that point and built a respectable book of business for someone at my level. But I felt that my early, modest success had been a function of sheer force of effort, not skill. I put hundreds and hundreds of hours every year into business development, and some of that effort paid off — but this model was not sustainable.

I engaged Steve hoping that his intensive training and coaching would help me accelerate the growth of my book with less time and effort. I wanted to develop business because I'd become good at it, not just because I tried hard.

My expectations were exceeded. I learned a tremendous amount from working with Steve, from grand philosophical insights to subtle, simple tactical moves. In the three years since my time with Steve, I've roughly tripled my book of business. I was elevated to become an equity shareholder in my firm. And I've been asked to lead the firm's program for training our upcoming associates in how to develop business. It is no exaggeration to say that Steve Fretzin changed my life.

One of my most treasured networking and referral relationships is with a brilliant business consultant named Dan. He's in his late fifties and has built an impressive network over his many years in business. Dan said to me once: "Neil, I have probably one hundred lawyers in my virtual 'Rolodex,' and you are one of about three of them who are worth a damn. I think the rest of them are just sitting in their offices, churning out billable hours, and hoping for the phone to ring." I was quite flattered by the compliment, but I also found it a sad commentary on the profession that I belong to and love.

So, dear reader: do you want to be one of the three out of one hundred lawyers who are "worth a damn" at networking? If you do, read on. Steve Fretzin's highly practical advice in this book is what you need to apply to get there.

Neil H. Dishman

Shareholder, Jackson Lewis P.C.

Chicago

Special Thanks

I'd like to express my special thanks to my wife Lisa, Kevin Ryan, Steve Shapiro, Lane Moyer, Neil Dishman, Sue Robinson, Sarah Victory, Dan Gershenson, Amy Gaber, Jeffrey Stahl, Thomas Field, Gary Levenstein, George Spathis, Doug Masters, Amit Mehta, Gregory Braun, Jordan Goodman, Bill Rudnick, Fred Tannenbaum, Carol Semrad, Linda McCabe, Katherine Hartrick, Bill Clayton and Kristine Tegelan.

Steve Fretzin

Introduction

Over the past 13 years, I've attended over 1,100 networking events and personally met with over 6,000 people while networking. The majority of these events were poorly run. The food was terrible, and I rarely met people who could do any real business with me. *So why did I continue networking?*

There are three simple answers to this question. First, I believed that networking, when done correctly, was the best way to build my business. Second, the most successful business people I knew told me to go out and network. Third, when I started building my business, I had no clients, so I had nothing to lose and plenty of time to devote to networking.

As a selling professional, I spent most of my career either cold-calling or working leads my company provided. My managers used to teach me "old school" sales techniques, which I hated using as much as the person on the other end of the phone hated hearing. I started networking to get away from the cold-call approach, but mistakenly thought that networking involved just showing up at events and passing out my business cards. For years I attended as many events and met as many new people as I possibly could. Back then, I couldn't have predicted the enormous amounts of time that networking would wrench away from my life. Furthermore, it took me years of making mistakes and wasting time to finally figure out how to get real value out of the time I invested.

The reality for many attorneys is that networking can be one of the best or one of the worst methods to expand their business. In the plus column, networking allows you to meet new people and prompts you to develop a "personal brand." But it also can be a colossal waste of time if it drains countless hours away from productive billable time or quality family time — not to mention that the return on investment can take a long time to realize.

All that being said, based on my own experiences and the results that I've seen with the hundreds of attorneys I've coached, I've concluded that networking is the best way, and possibly the only way, to truly grow your practice. Some people naturally love to network, while others despise it. What's true for all is that anyone and everyone can develop and improve on networking skills.

The philosophy behind this guide is to save you time, money, and energy by showing you how you can grow your legal practice through networking. The methodologies I've developed over the past 11 years have proven effective with new and experienced attorneys alike. Many of my clients have doubled, or even tripled, the size of their practices in less than a year. If you follow these strategies, you'll be sure to invest your time in networking activities more wisely, select the most productive opportunities to network, and meet with more qualified prospects than ever before.

As with much in life, it's about following a proven model versus just "winging it." My hope is that you'll follow my methodologies to grow your book of business with as little wasted time as possible. When you see the "takeaways" section located at the end of each chapter, be sure to note these important precepts to absorb and retain. They also provide a good summary of each chapter and make an excellent quick reference to return to after you've read the entire text.

I uncovered these business development methodologies in the traditional way — through trial and error. In truth, I don't know anyone who's made more networking mistakes than I have. The good news is that we rarely make the same mistake twice and that the best models, processes, and inventions were developed by the "trial and error" method. The ability to mess up, learn something, and improve as a result of that mistake is the cornerstone of professional development.

Please take advantage of the time I've invested and mistakes I've learned from to approach your goal of building meaningful business connections the right way, from the start. I'd say, "Good luck," but as you'll find as you read this book, luck has very little to do with becoming skilled at networking.

1

Where it all Begins: Being Positive and Forming Good Habits

I completely believe in the value of networking to build your practice, and I want to share with you simple ways to avoid making the same mistakes I've made. But I also don't want to sugarcoat or mislead you into thinking that networking is easy. While the process can be exhilarating, it can also prove to be exhausting. At some point, the thrill of meeting new faces and expanding your practice starts to wane. It's easy to get caught up in your day-to-day office routine and consequently put attention to networking on the back burner.

In working with successful attorneys who've developed robust practices, I've found that one constant among these professionals is the fact that they all understand the concept that business development never stops. Networking is a numbers game. For every 20 to 30 people you meet, there might only be 1 person with potential business or connections that are helpful for you. Read on for my secrets to keeping a positive attitude while stretching your comfort zone to make networking a part of your daily business routine.

There are three internal motivators that every successful networker must possess to succeed at networking: the right behaviors and habits, a positive attitude, and self-confidence. Without these internal drivers, it's nearly impossible to accomplish anything, let alone something as challenging as developing new business. This chapter is dedicated to helping you get into the proper mindset, which is important before we delve into networking methodologies.

It might seem rudimentary to talk about forming good habits and developing a positive attitude. After all, you wouldn't be a licensed attorney if you weren't able to implement good habits to study in law school and pass the bar exam. However, in my experience many attorneys overlook the importance of forming good habits when it comes to business development. I accept as the standard definition of behavior "a manner of acting or controlling oneself." Your behavior directly affects everything that happens in your life, including your income, your relationships, and your ultimate destiny. As you know, good habits can set you on positive paths while negative ones can cause you to veer off course. (1-A)

In business development, bad habits can have direct consequences on your ability to generate activity. Furthermore, poor habits can compound over time and confine you to the role of the law firm "worker bee," who is beholden to senior partners to bring in business. You wouldn't be reading this book if you were satisfied following that path.

A profound consequence of having negative behaviors and habits takes place subconsciously. Broken self-promises pile up and directly affect your general attitude and belief in yourself. Consider the behavior of putting off attending networking events using the "I'm too busy" excuse. Despite the best intentions, this behavior can all too easily continue indefinitely. The lack of follow-through can have a dramatic impact on your outlook toward networking. On the other hand, exhibiting positive behaviors creates good feelings and opportunities. (1-B)

However, breaking down your goal into components such as researching an upcoming event, registering for the event, and logging it on your calendar is a positive habit that will propel you forward to accomplishing your goal. Every time you commit to taking action and then actually follow through on that commitment, you're positively reinforcing winning habits. The positive experience creates momentum to continue this networking behavior in the future.

The secret of making, and keeping, a self-commitment is a key factor in why some people are more successful in accomplishing their goals than others. The small victories add up over time and reinforce the drive to continue good networking habits.

1-A

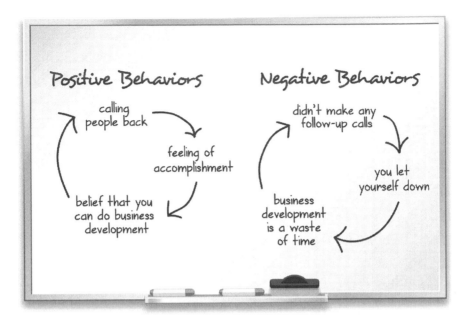

1-B

Developing "Strong Business Development Habits"

While it's easy to say that adopting positive behaviors will solve all your networking woes, there's certainly more to the art of becoming a successful networker than simply registering for one event. In his book THE POWER OF HABIT (2012), business reporter Charles Duhigg describes the key elements to changing poor habits. Duhigg categorizes three main components to any habit: cue, routine, and reward (1-C). For instance, when I was a teenager and into my twenties, I was a nail biter. Whenever I'd feel a sharp or extended nail on my finger (the cue), I'd put my finger in my mouth and bite it off (the routine), and then the nail was short and smooth (the reward). It took me years to figure out how to eliminate the bad habit, and it had to do mainly with changing the routine. What I did was to place rubber bands around my wrists. Then when I'd feel the sharp nail (the cue) and move to place the finger in my mouth (the routine), I'd see the rubber band and remember to snap the rubber band rather than putting my finger in my mouth. This method caused me to change the routine over time. Instead of the finger going into my mouth, I replaced the routine with a different, painful one. That had a powerful impact. I also bought five to ten nail clippers and kept them around me at home and in my office to ensure I had the proper tools handy to accomplish the reward of having a short and smooth nail.

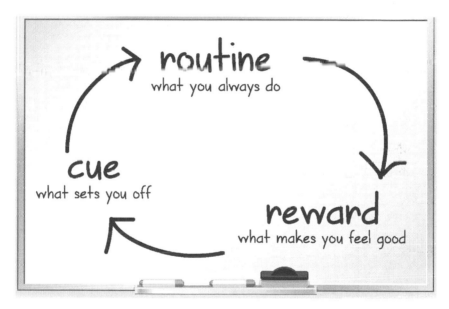

1-C
From The Power of Habit, Book by Charles Duhigg

This same principle applies to networking and business development. Make an effort to develop a routine of scheduling business development activities in the morning, before your day gets carried away with other matters. Try scheduling 30 minutes on a Monday or Friday morning to research events and make calls to schedule networking appointments. Not only will this routine help you get appointments, but it will also make you feel great the remainder of that day. If you recall, good behaviors equal positive attitudes.

Another approach is to look for the cue when you're tempted to avoid working on business development activities. For instance, you might notice that you feel overwhelmed when you see an event on your calendar, or that you feel disappointed when, at the end of the week, you realize that you've done very little to advance your networking. Either way, you should try to observe the possible cues and routines to identify the patterns and make efforts to change the routines. The best way to develop a routine to further business development goals is to schedule time to devote to it and to have a special reward in place once the task is completed. These are time-tested strategies to gain positive networking momentum.

Enjoying the "Swing of Networking"
Many lawyers avoid networking simply because they don't enjoy it. Over the years, I've heard many reasons, including, "It feels fake, like people are just meeting to see what they can get from you," "I didn't go to law school to do sales," and "I attended an event last night. What a waste of time that was." There are many reasons to dislike the actual "work" of networking; however, the way around these stumbling blocks is to learn to enjoy the process of networking.

For me, the game of golf has always been a bit of a roller coaster ride. Over the past 30 years I've butchered my share of tee boxes, fairways, and roughs without thinking seriously about improving my game. A few years ago I met Louis, a golf pro, and I decided to take a few lessons from him. What I didn't realize at the time was that I'd receive a lesson unrelated to golf that I hadn't anticipated.

When I met Louis at the range, he asked me to start the lesson by hitting a few balls so that he could observe my swing. After watching me step up and smash approximately ten golf balls into the field, Louis turned to me and said, "Do you enjoy swinging the golf club?" I paused for a moment, because I had no idea what he was getting at

"You seem to be approaching each shot with no purpose other than to get to the outcome as fast as possible," he said. "You don't seem to be enjoying your swing." I thought about that for a moment and then asked myself, "Do I really enjoy swinging a golf club, or am I just swinging aimlessly with the hope that I can land the ball somewhere near the green?"

A little reflection led me to realize that there was very little enjoyment for me in swinging a golf club. I was, in fact, rushing each shot too quickly just to get to the end result. If the sport of golf involves repeatedly swinging a golf club, but I'm not enjoying the swinging, then I had to ask myself, "Am I really enjoying the game of golf?"

Then it hit me that the true enjoyment of golf is in each individual swing. Proper attention to the techniques of setting up the swing and the actual movements involved in swinging the club are the factors that produce the best outcome. Thus, I'd found the missing piece of the puzzle to improve my game. I refer to this bit of wisdom gained as my "bonus lesson."

Why do we attend networking events? What's the underlying purpose for these gatherings? Most believe that there is new business to be found at networking events, while others view them as part of the importance of just "being out there." Whatever the case, we would all like to meet someone who can buy our services immediately.

As an attorney, your patience quotient for attending events and engaging in small talk may be very limited. Most likely, you're looking for the quickest result or to close the proverbial "deal" as soon as possible. It's natural that we'd all like to skip the chit-chat and move ahead to the nitty gritty, where we gain a new client and new business. While it's true that your numbers depend on "closing the deal," there's another important element that's key to your success in networking.

As a business development coach for attorneys, I'm always trying to find analogies to "teach" my clients about business development. Just like an unruly swing in golf, rushing through networking can lead to an unpredictable outcome. What if we focused on enjoyment of the swing in networking instead of focusing on the potential outcome?

Focusing on better planning and execution when networking will net the best value from your time investment. Instead of rushing through an event by pitching to or talking over the people we meet, we'd do well to slow the discussion down and ask thoughtful questions about our conversational partner's needs, interests, and even problems.

Few would argue that a "ready-fire-then-aim" networking model has little chance for effectiveness. The "enjoyment of the swing" of networking is to be found in the relationship and in truly getting to know someone when meeting that person for the first time. If you focus your energy there, the outcome is likely to be a successful one. Using this philosophy, you're freed up to enjoy the process of networking and leave behind the pressure to just go out and close the sale.

CHAPTER ONE TAKEAWAYS

- Building good networking behaviors by making commitments to yourself is key to finding success in business development.
- Positive behaviors affect your overall attitude. Honor the commitments you make to yourself just as you would the commitments you make to others.
- Developing positive habits will help you accomplish your networking and business development goals. Break a bad habit by noticing the cue and/or changing the routine.
- Focus on enjoying the process of networking rather than rushing through. Real relationships are built when you ask, listen, and understand another human being.

Networking Note

"You can't think in terms of what you're going to get back. The value is created when you help other people connect with whom they want to meet. And that value will come back to you — maybe not directly, and often in ways that you don't expect or even understand."

—BILL RUDNICK, DLA PIPER

2

Putting Yourself in the Right Place with the Right People

Before launching into the tactics of networking, it's important to have a good understanding of your ultimate goal. Whether you're a veteran or a novice at networking, it's important to go back to basics when looking to improve your results. Before running out the door to attend the next event that crosses your path, take a moment to stop and map out a strategic approach. Attending random events in a haphazard fashion may not be the best investment of your time, and your time is money. Before devoting time participating in any gathering, you should first define your target audience and determine the purpose for which you plan to meet them.

To be a productive networker, there are three main focus groups you should be targeting. The first group is the "direct buyers." These are individuals who personally need your services and who can make decisions to hire you to represent them. Second are the "strategic partners," who are those individuals conducive to serving as future sources of direct business referrals. The third group is comprised of "centers of influence." This group consists of well-connected individuals who may be able to refer you to buyers and strategic partners. (2-A)

Before attending the next event opportunity that presents itself, take a few moments to write down a profile of your best "prospective" clients, strategic partners, and centers of influence. For prospective clients, this list may include corporate presidents, chief executive officers, chief financial officers, and general counsel. For strategic partners and centers of influence, your list might include certified public accountants, wealth managers, bankers, attorneys, and executive consultants.

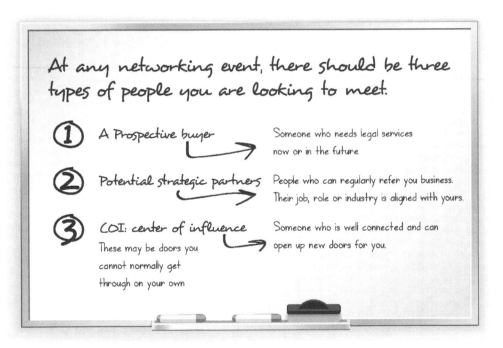

At any networking event, there should be three types of people you are looking to meet.

① A Prospective buyer — Someone who needs legal services now or in the future.

② Potential strategic partners — People who can regularly refer you business. Their job, role or industry is aligned with yours.

③ COI: center of influence — Someone who is well connected and can open up new doors for you. These may be doors you cannot normally get through on your own

2-A

12

If possible, research in advance the names of those individuals who'll be attending the event and ask yourself where these prospective attendees fit in with your list. One of the most effective ways to determine the potential for an event prior to attending is to speak with the event host. Contact the event organizer and ask a short list of pointed questions that will help you determine whether the event will be worth your time. For example, if you're keen to meet CEOs and CFOs, find out whether executives at that corporate level will attend. If you ask politely, the host may even give you an attendee list. This not only is a great tool to decide whether to invest your time at that particular event, but it can also serve as a list of potential contacts to follow up with afterward. Be forewarned and prepared to respond, however, for the event host or membership chair may try to sell you a membership to the group.

CHECKLIST OF PRE-EVENT QUESTIONS FOR HOST

- "What is the professional makeup of the membership or attendee list?"
- "When and how frequently are regular association or group meetings held?"
- "Are there any upcoming special events?"
- "How many attendees do you expect?"
- "How many attorneys attend your events?"
- "Are there any other related events that business owners might attend?"

- "Do you have any opportunities for members to present to the group as an educator?"
- "Does the organization have a committee structure? Are there other ways to become involved?"

Asking questions in advance and gaining a grasp of the makeup and goals of the organization will help you decide whether it makes sense to invest your valuable time attending one of these events. Disqualifying opportunities with little potential to put you in contact with people on your list will allow you to quickly move on to other networking opportunities that may be a better fit.

That being said, it's rare to meet CEOs and GCs at an "open" networking event. As an attorney looking for face time with these professionals, you might become frustrated to find that networking events you have access to aren't great for getting you in front of these decision-makers. Note that executives higher up the corporate ladder aren't likely to attend networking events due to the fact that that they're at a professional level where they have no need to network.

In reality, the CEOs and executives you want to meet may only be attending private golf outings and prestigious charity events. If you can gain entry to these circles, you're more likely to make lucrative connections as compared to those you might make at a general association meeting, for example. Therefore, you should always be prepared to primarily network with targeted strategic partnerships and centers of influence who have the potential to introduce you to those channels.

For example, a labor and employment attorney looking to reach human resources managers should focus efforts to meet others at networking events that are trying to make the same connections. This list might include payroll service providers, information technology companies, and health and wellness providers (2-B). Developing "lateral" strategic partners may be more valuable in the long run than meeting a direct business prospect. Consider the long-term effects of forging a relationship with a solid strategic partner who can refer multiple business prospects for ten years. That's an excellent return on investment.

Examples of Strategic Partners

Labor & Employment

Payroll Services

Information Technology

Health & Wellness Advisors

Estate Planning

CPA's

Financial Advisors

Transactional Attorneys

Real Estate

Bankers

CPA's

M&A Attorneys

Intellectual Property

Technology Consultants

M&A Attorneys

Marketing Professionals

2-B

Once you've identified your ideal prospects, take the time to research possible associations and events. The notion of networking with a room full of perfect strangers is daunting for anyone. It's critical to avoid negative self-rhetoric such as, "These events are a waste of time," "If I have one more bad breakfast...," or "Everyone I meet wants to sell me something." Remember, sometimes networking involves testing the waters to find out those lakes that aren't worth visiting.

TIPS TO EFFECTIVELY IDENTIFY POTENTIALLY WORTHY OPPORTUNITIES TO NETWORK

1. Ask referral sources, strategic partners, and colleagues whose business development skills you admire for their recommendations on the best avenues for finding prospects.

If you approach these skilled networkers with a genuine interest in learning from their experiences, they'll be more likely to share insights on those organizations they found to be fruitful.

2. Find out what organizations the "movers and shakers" in your field are involved with and research these associations, boards, and charities for potential opportunities.

If one organization seems crowded with competition, consider preferring others that may be lesser known but present more chances for you to make connections.

3. Identify and bookmark websites in the cities where you work and live that are dedicated to helping you find quality events.

For example, Crain's Chicago Business is a trusted authority on local Chicago business events. Visit its website, www.chicagobusiness.com, to find new prospects. Similarly, meetup.com posts a variety of meetings helpful to prospective networkers at www.meetup.com. Research and find the best websites dedicated to posting networking events that you can attend in your area.

4. Seek out organizations with which you share a personal interest or that has a commitment to serving a cause you support.

This might be a charitable organization, a hobby club, or an alumni group from your school days. You have a better chance of being motivated about attending and actually fitting in if you share a connection to a cause or interest.

Recently, I worked with a client who became involved with a local dog shelter not-for-profit helping to save dogs and find them new homes. Regularly volunteering at her local animal shelter and eventually joining the board has enabled her to "rub elbows" with many animal-centric business executives and veterinarians, who are the clients she seeks to serve in her legal practice. She's already picked up a few new clients as a result of her efforts on the board of an organization focused on a cause she's passionate about.

5. Try out a number of events before you make a decision to join one.

Many groups will allow you to visit a couple of times before making a decision to join. Use this "review" period to find out about the membership makeup and whether the organization presents quality opportunities to get to know your target connections and chances to become more involved with committees or subgroups. Testing the waters before committing to membership will help you make the best use of your networking time.

6. Know where your competition stands within the group.

Many groups you consider attending might already have one, two, or ten attorneys involved who are vying for the same business opportunities as you. This can be a sign either that you're in the right place or that you need to find another group to join. To find out, inquire as to how long your competition has been there, the quality of their reputation in the group, and whether they regularly attend the organization's events. Sometimes the "competition" isn't effectively working within the group and thus may not pose any real competition.

When you arrive at a new event, don't just focus on seeking out new clients. Instead, take the time to speak with other members to better understand the organizational landscape, which will help you gauge the competition and where you might fit in the organization.

A few years ago, I worked with a client who joined a group of over 30 practicing attorneys. However, there was only one other attorney who shared his area of concentration. As he became more involved with the organization, he learned that the other attorney was planning to retire within the next year. My client was able to obtain several connections because he was willing to take the time to learn about the organization and its members rather than retreating from a group that appeared at first glance to be teeming with other lawyers.

CHAPTER TWO TAKEAWAYS

- Create a master list of titles, professions, and types of people that you want to meet at an organization's event or as an active member of a group. Having this list in hand ahead of time will allow you to quickly disqualify events that won't include your primary targets. If time is important to you, it's worth being selective about the organizations with which you invest it.

- Find the right events to ensure you're starting off right from the beginning. Researching each association and event might be as simple as a five-minute conversation with someone who's attended before or five minutes browsing on the Internet and could potentially save you devoting hours or even years of your valuable time on a fruitless pursuit.

- Test a variety of groups and events to ensure you don't waste too much time in the wrong place. This may entail only one visit or possibly three or more to effectively survey the potential. Put in the effort to determine as quickly and efficiently as possible whether this opportunity is worthy of your time.

Networking Note

"The initial meeting and exchange of business cards is only a start — the key is following up. Developing a meaningful relationship happens over time and when you reconnect — multiple times and possibly on multiple levels through social media, e-mail, telephone calls, and in-person meetings. Set yourself apart from that pile of business cards by being proactive shortly after the initial meeting."

—KATHRYN M. HARTRICK, HARTRICK
EMPLOYMENT
LAW, LTD.

3

Developing a Constructive Networking Plan

Of the hundreds of attorneys I've worked with over the past 11 years, I've found that 95 percent don't have an effective, written plan for initiating the growth of their book of business. This is probably not a surprise; after all, drafting a business plan is not something most law schools teach students. But a networking plan is critical to your success. The adage "if you fail to plan, you plan to fail" is as true in terms of planning networking activities as it is in any other context. Devising a written plan focused on networking activities can save a tremendous amount of time, energy, and money.

To illustrate the importance of developing a networking plan, imagine we're planning a trip together through Africa. We'll start at the southernmost point of the continent and work our way north. If we were to decide to take off on this adventure without considering any future obstacles that may lie ahead, how long do you think it would be before we ran into trouble? If we failed to plan to meet predatory animals and militia groups and didn't bring proper provisions, we wouldn't have exactly created a blueprint for success. Now imagine we had the best very best GPS equipment available, an experienced guide, ample provisions, and plenty of protection to carry with us on this trip. Which approach would you prefer? (3-A)

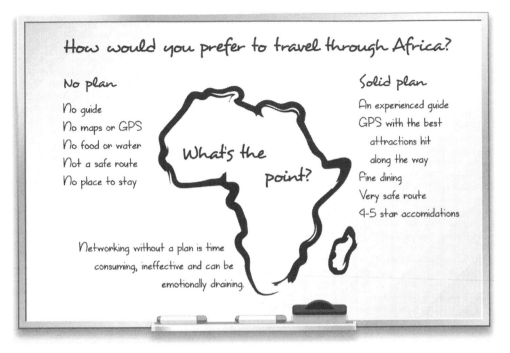

How would you prefer to travel through Africa?

No plan

No guide
No maps or GPS
No food or water
Not a safe route
No place to stay

What's the point?

Solid plan

An experienced guide
GPS with the best
   attractions hit
   along the way
Fine dining
Very safe route
4-5 star accomodations

Networking without a plan is time consuming, ineffective and can be emotionally draining.

3-A

Most people fail at networking and developing their book of business because they fail to plan. The focus of this chapter is writing a networking plan. By the time you've finished reading it, you'll be prepared to develop a time-conscious and roadblock-sensitive networking plan.

A networking plan should include the big-picture goals you want to accomplish over the next 12 months. It's imperative to break down this plan and your actions on a daily, monthly, and quarterly basis to ensure follow-through and, ultimately, success.

There are three primary steps to creating a networking plan. The first step is to identify your main objective. It should be phrased in terms of certainty that a specific goal will become a reality. It helps to state your goal in one concise sentence. For example, "I will have forged five new strategic partnerships by this June" or "I will have taken on five new matters by December 31st."

By writing your objective as a conclusory statement, you'll be reinforcing beliefs on a subconscious, as well as a conscious, level. If you know your business development numbers from the previous year, writing your objective should be easy. Set a high goal based on those numbers, but make sure it's still achievable considering your role within the firm and billable hours quota. Don't forget to factor in family time, which helps to provide a balance that makes you a more interesting conversation partner at networking events.

The second step in building a networking plan is to develop a series of concrete strategies. Once your networking plan objective is written, pinpoint two to five strategies drafted to help you accomplish your main objective. Examples include attending an industry-specific conference, joining an association, attending local events, or raising your profile on LinkedIn.

Make sure to begin by selecting strategies that are fairly easy to achieve and not too grandiose. For instance, if you focus your practice on a particular industry, it might make more sense to attend industry-specific events versus general-interest gatherings. An example of a strategy might be, "I will focus on developing my relationship with existing strategic partners at industry conferences in order to initiate quality introductions of at least two CEOs in the insurance field."

Once you've covered the first strategy, the next step is to identify opportunities that will provide the best chances of interacting with viable prospects and strategic partners. Rather than networking with other attorneys who, like you, are trying to develop business, you should focus on events and contacts that will increase your odds of eventually meeting with key decision-makers face-to-face. A decision-maker might be the CEO of a midsized manufacturing company, for instance. However, don't discount the possibility that another attorney may be a helpful strategic partner or even a client in need of your specific subject-matter expertise.

For instance, assume that your tactic to get started on the path you set up with your strategy is "I will research and attend two hospital administrator conferences this year." Another example of an effective strategy statement is "I will network directly with successful attorneys in the healthcare provider area to obtain quality introductions at the hospital administrator level." Force yourself to push outside your comfort zone to come up with the most effective strategies, and try to limit yourself to only a few solid strategies to ensure you'll meet your goals.

The third step in creating a networking plan is to pinpoint and write out specific tactics to ensure your strategies are properly executed. The most difficult part of developing new business is to effectively execute the strategies that you've outlined. The key here is to lay out the actions that will allow you to accomplish your networking strategies. Your tactics should provide a clear picture of how you'll invest your networking time and the results you expect from these efforts.

Try using the following guidelines for drafting tactics:

- Aim for several specific tactics for each strategy.
- Think of each of your tactics in terms of three stages: planning, execution, and follow-through.
- Another way to approach this plan is to treat each tactic as a story. Compose each with a beginning, middle, and end, and add these components underneath the tactic as bullet points.
- Each tactic should answer at least two of the following questions: "Who, What, When, Where, How, or Why." Take the time to actually ask yourself these questions as you're drafting your tactics. The more detail you include, the more actionable your tactics will be and the less likely you'll be to skip any steps.

SAMPLE ACTION NETWORKING PLAN

To help you better envision how a successful networking plan might look, here's an example of a strategy and corresponding tactics:

STRATEGY: **Network locally to obtain new business and develop new strategic partnerships.**

Tactic 1: **I will research local events and groups to determine where I should invest my time.**

- **I will speak with the top two attorneys at my firm to get their perspective on the groups with the most potential.**

- I will research industry-specific groups using Google, news authorities (*e.g.*, Crain's Chicago Business), and association websites seeking opportunities for local events I can attend.
- I will research the groups and associations of three attorneys I respect in my field to find out where they have been involved.
- I will contact four event or group hosts to discuss their association's and event's purpose.
- I will have this research completed and lists created by June 1.

Tactic 2: I will develop a personal "infomercial" as a mechanism to plan what I will say to contacts at these events.

- I will research different networking "scripts" and discuss ideas with top rainmakers in my firm.
- I will work on developing a niche for my practice and on focusing my infomercial to attract others who belong to that niche group.
- I will draft a script and practice it until I am comfortable.
- I will complete my script and be ready to deliver it by June 10.

Tactic 3: I will attend one event each month and obtain two or three promising connections from each event I attend.

- I will make sure to speak with four to six people at each event I attend.

- I will ask questions to better understand the contact's business, personal interests, or other areas of commonality.
- I will label each new contact's business card as an A, B, or C (based on potential as a new client or strategic partner). See Chapter 5 for more on classifying contacts.
- I will set follow-up expectations with each contact based on my rating of that contact.

Tactic 4: I will follow up with my A and B contacts after the event is concluded.

- I will reach out to those contacts I labeled as As and Bs by phone or e-mail within 48 hours of meeting these contacts.
- I will schedule a specific time on my calendar to make these follow-up calls or send follow-up e-mails.
- I will be prepared to discuss the event, common acquaintances, and meeting dates/places to build more rapport with the contact.
- I will request a meeting at a specific date and time at a quiet place with each contact.

While this sample plan should be tweaked to your personal strategy and tactics, it provides a basic outline for you to get started. Don't forget to define the who, what, when, why, and how of each tactic. Determining the when, a deadline for you to complete the task, is critical. Remember to be flexible and adjust the plan as circumstances dictate, but try to stay as close to the original plan as possible.

Working from a plan is always better than simply "winging it." Everybody needs a path to follow with confidence, just as when you use a GPS to find your destination or use a recipe to make a great meal. You can waste a lot of time shaking hands and having coffee without getting any closer to your business development goals. A plan keeps you positive and focused on specific tactics. This will keep your networking activities more productive.

CHAPTER THREE TAKEAWAYS

- Take the time to carefully draft a networking plan.
- Your networking plan should consist of strategies, which are goal statements.
- Every strategy should have concrete tactics, or action items, associated that answer who, what, when, why, and how you will employ each strategy.
- Stick to your networking plan closely, but don't hesitate to make the appropriate adjustments along the way if something isn't working the way you originally anticipated. This plan should be fluid, so that you don't get stuck with a strategy that isn't taking you in a positive direction.
- Track your progress. Keep the plan in front of you, and make a habit to review it daily. Check off or highlight things that you've accomplished to see your progress.

Networking Note

"When getting someone's card at a networking event, don't just glance at it and put it away. Take a good, hard look at it, and if possible comment on it. This shows genuine interest."

—JORDAN GOODMAN, HORWOOD
MARCUS &
BERK CHARTERED

4

Creating an Infomercial that Gets You Noticed

B efore heading out to conquer the networking world, it's important to have an effective infomercial or elevator pitch. An infomercial is your 30 – 60 second self-description, designed to help contacts understand what you do and how you may add value to them or people they might know.

Everyone should have something prepared to say to a group or individual when meeting for the first time. As in many areas of career development, "winging it" is not the best plan. Be ready to prepare a few different versions of your infomercial, as some situations may call for a longer, shorter, or altered version.

FOUR STEPS TO CREATING A MEMORABLE AND EFFECTIVE INFOMERCIAL

1. Include a statement of who you are and what you do.

The key here is to keep it simple; for example, "I'm an attorney focusing my practice on intellectual property, and I help people protect their trade names and patents." Or keep it vague; for example, "I'm an intellectual property attorney helping people to protect their valuable ideas."

2. Describe your prospect's pain points.

Instead of listing a bunch of features and benefits of your services, think of the pains that people may have that your services can alleviate. This is really important for a number of reasons. First, it allows you to stop bragging about yourself or your firm. Second, it's different than the typical "pitch" we've all heard before. Third, the concept of cutting straight to the negative or discussing problems people are having in their business gets people's attention. Try to use emotional words that capture the essence of the problem, issue, or frustration that people may have that you're able to help ease.

Think about the commercials for the cold remedy NyQuil, which is pitched as "the nighttime, sniffling, sneezing, coughing, aching head, fever, so-you-can-rest medicine." Can't you just visualize the on-screen patient in his pajamas, holding his head? Painting a vivid picture of the problem creates an effective and enduring image.

An example of a pain statement for an IP attorney is, "We typically help people who are unaware that their business name is at risk. What if you had to rebuild your respected brand all over again?" If you're speaking to someone to whom that scenario applies, they just might be interested in speaking with you further.

I try to throw out two or three pain statements relevant to my audience. You need to be flexible to tweak the message, depending on the recipient. The best practice is to identify the top two or three potential pain points and work with those. If you have a pretty good idea that at least one of these points will strike a chord with your target, then you've hit the mark. Most people either have legal issues themselves, or they know someone else who does. When leading with pain statements in your infomercial, people are more likely to accept that you have a solution for the issues simply because you've keenly identified them. Of course, be sure that you do actually have a solution to avoid an embarrassing situation.

3. Share your differentiator.

Create a "differentiator" for yourself or your practice. With the bombardment of media messages lobbed at us on a daily basis, it's more important than ever before to stand out from the crowd. Establishing and emphasizing an explanation as to how you or your firm is unique will help you attract the attention of potential clients and strategic partners. Ask yourself two questions to test whether your differentiator is effective. The first question is whether your message is different from any others you've heard, and the second question is whether this message is compelling enough to make someone really care about it.

Use your differentiator to separate yourself from the crowd of competition. For example, if you have a law firm policy that any incoming call that lasts under 15 minutes will not be billed, this is a potential differentiator from other attorneys. One word of caution, though: providing great service or a terrific quality product does not qualify as a differentiator. These factors do not make you unique, even if true. If others are saying the same thing, it doesn't pass the litmus test described above. If you're unsure how to identify a good differentiator, try asking former clients who've expressed a positive opinion of working with you. They may be able to shed some light on what makes you unique in the marketplace.

4. Make it easy for the group or individual to take the next step.

Be prepared with a statement that will help your target take the next step, such as, "If you're interested in hearing more about intellectual property practice and how my firm helps to protect our clients' interests, please see me after the meeting or visit my website at www.thecoolestIPguy.com." If you're speaking to an individual at an event, you might take more initiative and suggest a next step yourself by proposing a coffee meeting in the next couple of weeks to discuss a potential collaboration. Such a call to action is most natural at the end of a conversation.

These four steps virtually guarantee you have an effective message about the ways in which you help people and what makes you unique in the marketplace. You'll also become more memorable because you're forgoing the typical lawyer "feature and benefit" message, which is lazy, not to mention boring. Discussing the features and benefits of your practice can be viewed as boasting about yourself or your law firm and is an outdated approach to selling oneself. Remember to memorize your infomercial and practice delivering it with feeling and passion to make sure the message is confidently communicated.

The experience of an intellectual property attorney I helped a few years ago provides an example of the process of creating an infomercial. Those words that should be emphasized when delivering the message are italicized.

<u>Step 1:</u> I'm Dan Henry and I head up the intellectual property law group at Johnson & Adams. I've specialized in patents and trademark law for *over 20 years.*

Step 2: People usually come to me when a competitor accuses them of patent or trademark infringement, which can *handcuff* their business and *cost them thousands* or *sometimes millions* of dollars. Or they come to me when they learn that a competitor has knocked off their well-known product or name and is confusing their customers in the marketplace. This can cause *irreparable damage* to a business, resulting in lost sales and *wiping out* their reputation and goodwill that's taken decades to build.

Step 3: My clients love my proactive approach to protecting their intellectual property by asking the *really tough questions*. They tell me that no other practitioner has asked such in-depth questions to protect them.

Step 4: If you think your intellectual property, business name, or product could be at risk, please give me a business card before you leave today and I'll follow up with you. Thank you. Again, my name is Dan Henry with Johnson & Adams. (4-A) (4-B)

Be sure to keep your infomercial between 15 and 45 seconds, depending on the context of the conversation in which you're using it. Rarely will an individual want to listen to you ramble on for minutes at a time about yourself. This is an immediate turn off, as you probably know from the experience of listening to others. Write out your infomercial, practice it a dozen times, and then try it out without a script. Watch the listener's face for feedback. Make changes to ensure you're hitting the right buttons. Avoid memorizing verbatim, other than those words you've carefully selected to emphasize an idea, so you don't sound "canned."

Infomercial comparison.
Which would you rather listen to?

This one?

Hi, I'm Kevin Smith, a litigator with Thompson & Beck. I do civil litigation, commercial litigation, securities work, fraud cases and on occasion some appeals. We help our clients by providing great service at a reasonable fee. Happy to be of service to any of you if you need this kind of work. Thank you.

or

This one?

I'm Kevin Smith and I'm a partner in the litigation group at Thompson and Beck. Clients typically come to me when they have business-related headaches and are unsure how to address them. For instance, I frequently counsel my banking clients when they're concerned about aggressive debtors threatening to tie them up in litigation, or when they've realized they have errors in their loan documents that could cost them thousands. I've seen clients go crazy trying to sort these problems out, throwing good money after bad.

I make sure my clients know that they can reach out to me day or night. In addition to sharing my cell phone number with all my clients, I make sure they also have my home number for emergencies. If you're ever in a position where you're concerned about a potential or actual dispute, please contact me, and maybe I can be of assistance. I'm always willing to take a call and serve as a "sounding board." Thank you for your time. My name is Kevin Smith with Thompson and Beck.

4-A

Infomercial comparison. Which would you rather listen to?

This one?

I'm Kevin Smith and I'm a partner in the litigation group at Thompson and Beck. Clients typically come to me when they have business-related headaches and are unsure how to address them. For instance, I frequently counsel my banking clients when they're concerned about aggressive debtors threatening to tie them up in litigation, or when they've realized they have errors in their loan documents that could cost them thousands. I've seen clients go crazy trying to sort these problems out, throwing good money after bad.

I make sure my clients know that they can reach out to me day or night. In addition to sharing my cell phone number with all my clients, I make sure they also have my home number for emergencies. If you're ever in a position where you're concerned about a potential or actual dispute, please contact me, and maybe I can be of assistance. I'm always willing to take a call and serve as a "sounding board." Thank you for your time. My name is Kevin Smith with Thompson and Beck.

4-B

A few years ago, I had an estate-planning client who attended one of my networking events. When it was his turn to speak, he used these four steps in addressing the group. He referenced the "tragedy and pain" that children endure when both partners of a couple die without an estate plan, facing the prospect of the court deciding their fate, for better or worse. At the end of the meeting, my client had three people lined up to take his business card to set up a meeting about their estates. It's amazing how people react to a well-written and executed infomercial.

CHAPTER FOUR TAKEAWAYS

- While there are literally thousands of models for a good infomercial, I've found that the one I've shared with you has a little of everything that people want to hear because

- it prompts you to convey your message without verbally overwhelming the listener;

- it provides specific examples of legal issues or "pains" your audience can relate to and visualize;

- it shares what's different about you that others can't or don't say; and

- it implies a next step to move someone forward to a future meeting with you.

Networking Note

"When networking in a group setting, listen first and add value to the conversation by asking open-ended questions. This will ensure your commentary will add to, not subtract from, the conversation."

—AMIT MEHTA, PAUL HASTINGS

5

Generating Success at New Networking Events

Entering a room to attend a new networking event can be very intimidating. Whether the room contains 20 new faces or 200, many attorneys struggle with the idea of walking into this unknown situation. I can empathize with these feelings, as it's daunting to me as well. Fortunately, with proper preparation and a plan of action in place, these fears can be minimized. In this chapter, I share some proven steps that will help you navigate a new event and get you more comfortable in your approach:

1. Before attending any networking function, solidify your image/personal brand for your audience.

You get only one chance to make a first impression, so make it count. If you want to be seen as a professional in your field, be sure to always dress at the same level or, better yet, one step above the other participants. Showing up in jeans to an event where everyone is dressed "business casual" is frankly unacceptable if you aim to be taken seriously by others. While this might seem obvious to most career-conscious individuals, many people continue to show up to professional events looking less than appropriate.

Most of us have heard the adage "never judge a book by its cover." If you ask any successful book publisher, they'll tell you that a book's cover is an important component in the buying process. The reality is that most people make up their minds about someone new within the first 20 seconds of meeting that person. Well-groomed hair, ironed clothes, eye contact, a smile, and a firm handshake can make all the difference when meeting new people. Don't forget those breath mints, either. (5-A)

New Event Checklist

☐ I've researched and vetted the event to ensure it's right for me.

☐ I know that the attendees are made up of possible prospects, strategic partners or centers of influence.

☐ I've made efforts to connect with the people running the event to facilitate introductions made when I arrive.

☐ My infomercial is prepared and well rehearsed.

☐ I look good! My hair, nails, breath and clothes will all be received well.

☐ My attitude is positive! I'm feeling good about myself, and the prospect of meeting some solid people.

☐ I have a goal set to collect 5-8 cards and follow-up with 2-3 of them within 48 hours.

5-A

If you're not sure how you look or come across to others, ask your spouse or colleague to be totally honest with you. It's important to be open to constructive criticism to ensure that you're not turning people off due to factors you can easily fix.

2. Do your homework and know who the "key players" are in the room.

If you're investing your valuable time to attend an event, reach out and call the event organizer or anyone you know who's involved with the group. Be prepared with questions to uncover who'll be there who might be of value to you, and go ahead and ask for a guest list. Upon arrival, try asking the host to introduce you around to a few key people. The organizer likely has a stake in your positive experience to ensure the event is a success.

3. Once you've arrived, look for people standing alone, rather than people standing in a group of three or more.

If it's your first time at a new event, try to seek out people who have a *handwritten* name badge. This can be an indicator that they're new to the group. This commonality can build instant rapport with them. All you have to do is walk up to the person and ask, "Is it your first time here, too?" If it is, they'll feel great relief in meeting someone else who's new to the group. If they've been there before, you can mention the handwritten name badge and turn the conversation to that person's experience with the event or association.

At a cocktail or dinner event you might try hanging out at the bar and speaking to people as they queue up to get a drink. Take note of their name badges, including the business names, and then ask them about their work. You also might start a conversation based on their choice of drink.

4. Meet someone new and then build on that connection to meet others at the event.

Another tip regarding working a room is to try to work with the people you've already met to meet those you haven't. For example, if you've spent some time getting to know a CPA, you should ask that individual to introduce you to other people he knows at the event. If you did a good job explaining whom you're looking to meet, the CPA should be happy to make introductions.

The best way to work a room is to not be a stranger for very long. Between the people running the event and the new people you meet, build on your "starter relationships" to continue making new connections. Pretty soon, you've made three to five solid connections, and you can consider the event a success.

5. Remember that "networking" has the word "work" in it for a reason.

Remember the real reason you're attending networking events. It's not for the purpose of eating, drinking, and socializing, but rather to establish meaningful business relationships. Go there with a plan to meet and follow up with at least three to five new contacts. Think about whom you'd want to meet prior to attending and then focus on seeking out those people.

For example, if business consultants and wealth managers have traditionally been effective referral sources for you, focus on trying to meet new people with these credentials. Don't overlook the possibility that someone who doesn't fit those criteria probably knows someone who does. Remember to look for connections the person with whom you're speaking may have with others. For all you know, a small business owner you're talking with might sell services to wealth managers and know the most connected ones in the area. He or she could be a great referral source for you.

A big part of "working" a networking event is in asking the people you meet about their business. I try to do this right away to ensure that I can tailor my infomercial or elevator speech to best connect with their needs. For example, consider walking up to a person, looking at their name badge, and then saying, "Hello, _____, my name is _____ . What do you do?" Once he or she responds, you can follow up with thoughtful questions such as, "How did you get your start in the _____ business?", "What do you enjoy most about your profession?" or "What are some of the changes that have occurred in your industry?"

If you find yourself dominating the conversation, try to ease up. It's far more important to learn about your new acquaintance than to talk about yourself. Listen to the person and try not to become distracted or start looking around the room. Your eyes, ears, and body language should be focused on the person with whom you're conversing. Giving that person your full attention demonstrates that you care, which could set up a powerful long-term relationship. Skimming the crowd with your eyes shows a lack of respect for the person you're with.

6. Try to find natural affinities or commonalities with your contact.

When you're asking questions, look for opportunities to capitalize on common ground with your interlocutor. This might be the university that you both attended, or maybe you both have a passion for tennis. Whatever the topic, commonalities provide a framework to build rapport around. This can be one of the easiest ways to build trust and eventually lead to discussion of the contact's legal issues or needs, which might surface much more quickly once there's a bit of trust established.

One word of caution here is to beware of falling prey to one-upmanship, which is the phenomenon of trying to tell a better story than the last person speaking. For example, if someone discussed a car crash he was involved in, I'd step in and one-up him with my story of my airplane crash. People love to tell stories, but can feel marginalized when a reply seemingly dismisses their experience. A better bet is to listen to their story and empathize with their situation. If you have a better story to share, downplay it to ensure it doesn't overshadow the other speaker's experience.

7. Don't forget that connections are everywhere.

In my experience, the average person has between 200 and 500 people in their immediate network. Therefore, the people you meet while networking should have plenty of possible contacts to share if they have the desire or the abil-ity to connect you with them. Even if someone isn't a clear fit to work directly with you, there still might be benefits to developing a relationship with that individual.

Once when I was networking at a local chamber, I was speaking with a charming young lady who was selling cosmet-ics. In addition to the fact that I have no personal need for cosmetics, I just couldn't imagine how she could possibly be a good connection for me. Needless to say, I hung out with her for 10 – 15 minutes listening about her business successes and failures. I stayed focused, was a good listener, and demon-strated a high level of empathy for her situation. (I believe that feeling understood is one of our most basic human needs.) Near the end of our discussion, she asked me what I did for a living. I shared my 30-second infomercial with her and could practically see the wheels turning in her head. Once I finished, she told me about her husband's company and its sales woes. An introduction was eminent, and my "cosmetics connection" ended up leading to one of my biggest new clients that year.

8. Know when to walk away.

On the flip side, I've had countless experiences at events with people that didn't go quite so well. In taking five to ten minutes to speak with someone, I've found

- the rude
- the boring
- the egomaniacal
- the overly salesy

- the selfish
- the greedy
- the vain
- the incessant talker
- the taker
- the sloppy drunk
- the crazy
- the unintelligent
- the lost soul
- the outrageous

I've even had someone tell me to get a job because my business model wouldn't work.

These are some of the people we need to hear from, if for no other reason than to avoid them moving forward. Everyone you meet is worth at least five minutes of your time, even if that time is used simply to disqualify that person as a potential strategic partner or prospect. Moving someone to the "no" column saves time for both you and the contact, as there'll be no follow-up required.

Who hasn't been stuck in a conversation that leaves you practically squirming to end it? I've found that the easiest and most polite way to end a conversation is to excuse yourself to go to the restroom. I've tried escaping to the bar before, only to be followed. Another option is to be straightforward with the other person and say, "It's been nice talking with you, Fred. I promised myself that I'd meet at least three new people at this event today, so I'm going to circulate. Please excuse me." Then walk away and don't look back.

Early on in my networking experience, I found myself in a conversation with a life insurance salesman who was a clear "no" for me in terms of a promising connection. After listening to him talk "at" me for over 15 minutes, I decided to be bold and take the opportunity to try to help him with his networking skills, which clearly needed work. I explained to him that, in my experience, networking events are not the best venue to "sell" your services and that he might want to try asking people questions and getting to know people first. The salesman seemed genuinely grateful for my quick coaching tip, so I decided to invite him to attend one of my business development classes. He attended the following week and met a number of my successful clients. He also managed to finagle away all of my clients' business cards. He then proceeded to call and hound my clients for business. As you can imagine, my clients were less than pleased with me, not to mention this disingenuous salesman.

For me, this was a valuable learning experience. It drove home for me how important it is to "qualify" someone before offering up a referral, or in my case providing him access to many of my clients. There are rare occasions in which some people shouldn't be helped and even should be actively avoided.

9. Learn and use the ABCs of networking.

One easy-to-implement strategy is to literally "rate" the people that you're meeting at these events. After briefly speaking with someone at a networking event, and then receiving that person's business card, take ten seconds as you walk away to rate that individual as a potential prospect or strategic partner by jotting an A, a B, or a C (or a number sequence you've worked out ahead of time) on the back of the person's business card. Your "grade" on the card represents how quickly you should follow up with that person. Be sure to exercise caution when assigning your rating and do so after you've left the conversation. It wouldn't take much for a person to figure out that the not-so-discreet letter C you wrote on his or her card represents your assessment of him or her after a few minutes of conversation.

Whether you choose to use a letter or number system, the evaluation system you use to classify those people you connect with at events should include the following categories.

An A grade represents the "cream of the crop," those individuals who may directly need your services or who might become a beneficial strategic partner for you. For those contacts you classified with an A, you should make sure to follow up within 24 hours of the event. If you're able to work it in, these people are worth trying to schedule a coffee meeting with for the following week, even while you're still chatting at the event. As long as it makes sense for both parties, the sooner you book a meeting, the better.

The Bs are those individuals you'd like to get to know better or at least continue the conversation with by telephone to determine whether there's a possible connection. Follow up with these contacts within 48 hours of meeting.

Lastly, there's the C category, which is for those people who don't appear to be a connection you think worth pursuing. This isn't to say that no connections can be made with your C acquaintances, but you'll want to make sure that, if you agree to meet with a C, the person is someone with whom you had a successful initial conversation. Use as your barometer the value of your time to determine whether you should follow up with this person.

Don't feel that you have to say "yes" to an additional meet up with every contact you come across at the networking events you attend. However, keep in mind that you might be more open to following up with people when you start networking than when you've established more connections. When I started networking and had few contacts, I was much more open to following up with those C people I met to see where that connection might possibly lead. Once I began building my network with the right people, meeting a second time with Cs became a real challenge for my time and my patience. It can be challenging to have a meaningful networking exchange with someone who isn't really able to help you or vice versa. Meeting people just for the sake of meeting is not usually time well spent.

With respect to your As and Bs, it's imperative that you follow up quickly. New deals and strategic partners can be lost due to poor follow-up skills. If you have a stack of business cards on your desk awaiting contacts right now, that's a big no-no. These cards should be processed and calls made as soon as possible. Think of it this way: you've made the reservation at a five-star restaurant, bought the ring, and have champagne chilling. Are you going to drop the ball with the proposal? Following up is *the* most important element of all in successful networking.

When you do schedule a meeting, try to find a quiet meeting space that will allow both you and your contact to focus on the conversation. Your private office or the contact's office are good options. A quiet hotel lobby can also work, especially if you're traveling. Although it's sometimes inescapable, try to avoid meeting at bustling coffee shops like Starbucks because they're not conducive to communication. Between blenders whirring and multiple conversations swirling, it's extremely easy for you and your contact to become distracted. Whenever possible, you want to have your new friend's full attention and to provide yours in return.

10. Perhaps the very best question to ask a new contact when you're networking is "What should I be listening for in a good referral for you?"

While there are many questions that should be asked when meeting someone new at an event, this important question accomplishes a few critical things. First, it's a sign of generosity that you've shown interest in helping someone else. Second, it's a very professional question that is rarely asked by even the most experienced networkers. Third, it shows genuine interest in helping someone to find key referrals, which builds trust. While accomplishing all of these things, it doesn't commit you to taking immediate action. Remember, you asked "What should I be listening for," which demonstrates interest without making an actual commitment to provide an introduction.

While we do want to help people, we need to ensure that we know the person much better before executing on any real introductions. Remember, you've only known this person for five to ten minutes. Instead of providing a referral on the spot, take note on his or her card or in your head about referrals that might be appropriate. Just don't share them out loud yet. If you decide to meet for coffee sometime and feel good about the person's business acumen, a referral might be the perfect next step.

CHAPTER FIVE TAKEAWAYS

- Working the room doesn't have to be a chore. If you go in with a plan and have a little process to what you're doing, your time will be more wisely invested.
- Preparation before networking can make all the difference.
- Make it a point to ask a lot of questions, especially the "most important" question about how you can help your contact.
- Finding commonalities is the key to building rapport.
- Don't talk about yourself too much.
- Gathering information and business cards for new contacts is far more valuable than chatting up everyone you meet and handing out your cards.
- By following these suggestions, you'll gain valuable insight into which individuals are worth following up with and you'll be better received by your new contacts.

Networking Note

"You never know who will be an important contact in your future — an associate at your firm, your neighbor's daughter, a student in your law school class. Look for ways to connect with people and help them any way you can."

—DOUGLAS MASTERS, LOEB & LOEB LLP

6

Getting Results when Working a Conference

There are hundreds of professional conferences annually that are attended by hundreds of thousands of attorneys. These events can be time consuming and expensive and in the end net little to no actual new business for attendees. Considering all those factors, it seems to defy logic that anyone still goes. But just as is the case with any business-building platform, there are ways to improve your odds that things will go your way.

The value of most conferences is realized by the best-prepared participants. Devising a plan to be added to the agenda as a presenter, obtaining an attendee list in advance, and making a point of scheduling coffee meetings with prospective attendees prior to the conference are a few of the insider tips on which this chapter focuses. With a well-thought-out plan in advance, proper execution, and prompt follow-through, you can change the ho-hum conference experiences in your past into a fertile ground for cultivating new business prospects.

Think back to the most recent conference you attended. Did you say or even think to yourself any of the following statements before, or even after, the event:

- "This is probably going to be (or was) a waste of time."
- "The room will probably be (or was) wall-to-wall with lawyers."
- "Thank goodness I'm getting (or I got) CLE credit, or this event would be (or would have been) of no value at all."
- "I hope my presentation will go (or went) well and will get (or got) someone's attention to lead to future business."
- "At least I can (or could) count on visiting with some of my colleagues and friends."
- "It will be (or was) nice to get out of the office for a few days."
- "This is (or was) a great opportunity to collect lots of business cards. I really need to follow up with the people I met."

Here's a question for all the litigators out there. Would you willingly head to trial without preparing first? Of course not. Just as there are tried-and-true trial preparation tactics you learned in school and on the job, there are some key "success elements" to obtaining new business from attending professional conferences.

Success Element #1: Develop a solid pre-conference plan or strategy.

The components of this plan might include

a. background research on past conferences to determine which sessions and/or receptions might include the best prospects for new clients or strategic partners you'd like to meet;

b. a thorough review of the guest list, if you can obtain it in advance, in order to understand the background of the attendees (Review the list and place a check next to the people you most want to meet.);

c. pre-event meetings (breakfast, lunch, or drinks) with some of the prospective attendees (Reach out proactively by telephone or e-mail to schedule these meetings so you'll have a context in place before the event.);

d. discussions with peers, colleagues, and/or friends who've attended the same (or a similar) conference in the past to get the "inside" scoop on the opportunities available;

e. conversations with the event organizer to get more information about the meeting and to arrange introductions when attending (This can pay big dividends if that person is open to helping you connect at the conference.);

f. goals for the number contacts you plan to meet each day (Be aggressive with your numbers to ensure you'll meet enough people with whom you'll actually want to follow up after the event.);

g. your completed and well-studied infomercial or elevator pitch to ensure you're seen as focused and polished (See Chapter 4 for guidance on creating your personal infomercial.);

h. a list of relationship-building and business-focused questions to ask those you meet; and

i. practice role-playing to ensure you're ready to ask effective questions that can lead to the development of strong relationships.

Success Element #2: Prepare to execute your plan at the event.

Thorough planning before the conference matters, but just as important is the next element — execution. When conference day arrives, you'll want to avoid becoming a wallflower or shrinking violet. No matter how introverted you might be, it's critical that you show up and perform with energy. Advance preparation makes this level of interaction more comfortable and natural. Luckily, there are several tips you can implement to increase your "performance" at any conference:

When meeting someone new, always be the first one to begin asking questions. In the beginning, you should focus on listening to your contact and learning more about this individual. The more quickly you take in meaningful data, the more quickly you can quickly determine if this person is someone you want to invest more time with or if you'd be better served by moving on and meeting others.

At some point during your conversation, it might be appropriate to ask your new contact if any of his or her colleagues at the conference might be interested in meeting you. Sometimes the person you're talking to may be better suited to connect you to a prospect than to become an actual prospect. Try to understand your contact's business role, position level, and circle of influence. These factors can prompt the contact to effectively introduce you to his or her contacts. In addition, your contact may know about a cocktail reception or other similar event that could put you in a room of possible prospects that you never would have met otherwise. Be open to connections this contact can facilitate.

Don't let a good contact slip away. If you meet someone who strikes you as interesting, well connected, or a prospective client, be sure to get his or her card. Try to make arrangements with this person later. You could do so by saying "It was really nice meeting you and hearing about all that you do. If you're open to it, I'd really like to meet again and discuss ways we might be able to help one another. How about breakfast tomorrow?" If the individual isn't available, make sure you collect all of the person's contact information so you can follow up accordingly.

Schedule as many quality meetings with other attendees as possible. You're not building your book of business when you're in your hotel room watching bad movies. Look at the one to three days that you're there, and commit any free time to holding more one-on-one meetings.

Just as when attending any networking event, label your collected business cards with an A, a B, or a C to ensure that you remember whom you met that you thought might be most valuable to your network. This also will help ensure follow-up with the As and Bs directly after the conference.

Connect with your new friends on LinkedIn. This will help you better understand each new contact's background and who else they know. This little step can make your follow-up meetings even more interesting.

Schedule follow-up calls with attendees before you leave the conference. If you're speaking with someone and it makes sense to speak again, pull out your calendar and schedule the time while that contact is right in front of you. This is better than getting back to them when they might be too busy to take your call.

Speak to the people sitting next to you at each meal and workshop. Sometimes the best opportunities happen when you least expect it. You can easily double or triple your chances of meeting a valuable connection just by doing this one thing.

Success Element #3: Seize your window of opportunity after the conference.

The third element of being successful at a conference happens after you leave. Remember that, when developing new business, you typically have a short *48-hour window* to follow up in order to get the best possible results. You'll need to get moving straight away when you return to the office.

Some of my attorney clients will wait weeks before making follow-up phone calls. Don't leave to chance that your new contact has a good memory; you can lose the chance to make a connection with even those who do once they get back to their "daily grind."

Additionally, communicating early is important because the energy of the conference is still fresh for your prospects. If you're looking for one way to help make a follow-up call or e-mail stick, say the following to a valuable connection before leaving the conference: "I'd really like to follow up with you again to continue this conversation. Is it best to reach you through e-mail or just to call?" This way you also ensure you'll be touching base using the contact's preferred manner of communication. (6-A)

SUCCESS TACTICS FOR FOLLOWING UP WITH POTENTIAL STRATEGIC PARTNERS

- Review the person's LinkedIn profile to see your second-degree and his or her first-degree connections. This will help you better qualify possible introductions you might ask your new contact to make. See Chapter 14 for more information about using LinkedIn as an effective networking tool.
- Develop questions to better understand the individual's business, including your contact's target market. Try to think of connections you could foster for this new acquaintance. Always remember that networking is a two-way street.
- Ask questions to understand whether meeting face-to-face or by telephone to follow up makes more sense. Disqualifying potential contacts is just as important as qualifying them, and doing so can conserve your valuable time.
- Set a "loose" agenda for your next meeting to ensure both parties will get value and walk away with concrete plans to help one another.

Make your own luck at any conference

Typical Approach

- No thought before the conference
- No list requested or reviewed
- I was a wallflower at the conference
- I left the event with a stack of business cards ...They've been sitting on my desk for weeks!

New Approach

- Reviewing this chapter six weeks before attending a conference
- List of attendees and speakers was reviewed prior to the conference. I connected with 5-10 people to set up coffee/drink meetings
- I made an effort to speak with more people. Especially the people sitting to my left and my right at each presentation
- I labeled the cards A, B & C. I followed up with all the A's and B's within 48 hours.

6-A

SUCCESS TACTICS FOR FOLLOWING UP WITH PROSPECTIVE CLIENTS

- LinkedIn is an excellent tool for following up with new contacts. Look for common first-degree connections to determine connections you have in common. This helps with relationship building and finding natural affinities. See Chapter 14 for more on this topic.
- Take a few minutes to develop rapport. It's fine to talk about the conference or acquaintances you may have in common with this person. Hopefully, you jotted

some quick notes about your new connections while still at the conference so that you have topics to chat about afterward that you can tie back to your initial conversation. For example, compare notes with your contact about who you thought was the best conference speaker or which was the best reception you attended.

- When you get to the phone call, be alert for, and even gently probe for, any legal issues or problems with existing vendors your prospect might be having. Anytime someone shares this type of information with you, this is an opening for you to move forward and help the person improve the situation. If you do identify problems, you could ask what issues in particular are causing the contact and his or her company the most frustration. Make sure you know he or she is interested in discussing this with you before asking this question.

- Schedule a full meeting during this follow-up call. The goal isn't to "close a sale," but rather to gain commitment to the next step: a full meeting.

- Try to understand whether your contact is a decision-maker for the company or newer counsel. If not, ask subtle questions about the contact's business to find out who the decision-makers are.

- Set an agenda for your meeting. This will set up the meeting to accomplish both your goals and those of your contact.

CHAPTER SIX TAKEAWAYS

- There's only one way to work a conference effectively — preparation.
- Conferences and networking events can be an excellent source of business contacts when managed properly.
- Don't squander the opportunity conferences present by simply signing up and attending with little to no direction.
- Develop a networking conference plan by setting goals and planning strategies you'll employ at the event.
- Execute your plan and follow up like a true professional to improve your success at an event or conference.

Networking Note

"No matter how hard you try, you must accept the reality that the majority of the people with whom you network are not capable of building a working relationship that will be mutually beneficial. You must trust your instinct and be prepared to move on if the fit is not right. Your time is better leveraged by thoughtfully pursuing fewer promising opportunities than it is by attempting to exhaust every opportunity you come across."

—GEORGE SPATHIS, LEVENFELD
PEARLSTEIN, LLC

7

Paying Your Networking B-I-L-L

As we've established already, asking your contacts questions is essential to networking success. Resist the urge to "talk yourself up" and remember that you'll be more interesting when you listen than when you talk, and people will generally like you more. Keep in mind the "80/20 Rule" for business development conversation: you should spend 80 percent of a conversation listening and only 20 percent of the time speaking. We have two ears and one mouth for a reason. Keep your use of each proportionate.

Have you had the experience of walking into a crowded networking event that seems to be buzzing with energy, looking around in amazement at all the people engaging in conversations, and wondering what they all could possibly be talking about? After about five minutes of standing around and watching nervously in this situation, you'll realize that you should become involved in the action. How can you comfortably join the mix at this event? What questions should you ask people? How can you have personal and lasting impact on the people with whom you speak? Tap into your "inner reporter" and ask these individuals questions about themselves.

I've developed a simple acronym for recalling the best topics to discuss during networking events. It is always a good idea to "pay the B-I-L-L" when developing new relationships. The term "B-I-L-L" will help you remember the key topics you should try to focus on when making conversation with a new contact. Each letter stands for a topic: "B" for business, "I" for interests, "L" for loved ones, and "L" for life purpose.

Business: Ask questions about the person's business.

After approaching someone and finding out his or her name, open up the conversation by asking your new contact questions about himself or herself. Be curious and be on the lookout for common interests, or "natural affinities," you share with this person. If you're at a networking event, asking questions about the individual's business is a logical discussion topic. You can ask this casually, simply by asking your new contact what business he or she works in. Because this question is expected, it's a neutral starting place to open a dialogue with a new person.

You can expand on this topic by asking how the individual came to be in his or her particular line of work, and then ask additional questions to gain an understanding of the person's history. If your "career story" shares common elements with this new contact, you have a natural affinity to build rapport on. This topic can also give you a sense of the contact's experience and insight into his or her professional background and perspective.

A way to extend this discourse even further is to ask what the contact enjoys most about his or her business. Try to discover his or her passion. Again, you should search for commonalities between you and your newly made friend.

The flip side of asking about the joys of business is to inquire into the professional frustrations your contact has encountered or is currently dealing with. This is an important question, because it opens the door to uncovering a problem you might have the potential to help this person fix. If it's clear that the person doesn't have an issue that you could assist with immediately, perhaps you know someone else who'd be able to help this contact, which can move your new relationship forward via altruism and build trust through offering assistance without the implication of any personal gain on your part.

Interests: Inquire into the person's interests.

It's human nature to enjoy talking about our personal interests and hobbies, which is why you can't go wrong when asking what a person does for fun. According to an article in Scientific American, a Harvard University study measured blood flow of subjects who were talking about themselves and determined that thinking and talking about oneself increases neural activity and indicates an "intrinsic reward" that a person experiences and that increases with the addition of an audience. See Adrian F. Ward, *The Neuroscience of Everybody's Favorite Topic*, Sci. Am., July 16, 2013, www.scientificamerican.com/article/the-neuroscience-of-everybody-favorite-topic-themselves.

Whether your contact's chosen hobby is fishing or golf, all you have to do is open the door and allow the person to talk about the interest. Try to find natural affinities, but don't force them. Even if you don't share outside interests, you can still build rapport by being an active and interested listener, thereby creating a positive association with your contact.

In the same vein, questions about someone's background are typically well received. Discussing someone's hometown or current city is a great way to build rapport. There are all kinds of great conversations that can stem from this simple question. Follow up by asking what the individual likes best about the area he or she lives in or came from. The person's alma mater is also a positive conversation prompt that can lead to more connections, either firsthand or third-party. Whether your contact chooses to discuss the local high school, the University of Illinois, or Harvard Law School, listen and ask more follow-up questions.

These background questions afford you the opportunity to learn about connections you may have in common with the new person — neighbors, former classmates, and family and friends — which leads to the first "L" of our acronym: loved ones.

Loves ones: Talk about the person's loved ones.

Asking whether the person is from the "area" is an organic lead-in to discussing family-oriented topics. Be cautious when it comes to inquiring about the person's marital status or length of marriage due to the sensitive nature of the question. Be observant before asking and notice whether the contact appears to be wearing a wedding ring as well as the person's apparent age. However, this topic can help you steer the conversation toward revealing information that exposes natural affinities with you. For example, if the person mentions being married for 25 years and you've been married for just 2, if you can do so with sincerity you could ask for secrets on how to keep a marriage strong for so many years.

When discussing children, it's best to wait for your contact to take the lead as to that subject. If the contact mentions children, have at it; this is an excellent way to bond with someone new. However, you should proceed with extreme caution, as this can be a sensitive subject to people who don't have children but wanted them or individuals who've lost a child. Once the door is open, though, a tactic to keep up the conversation and find commonalities with the contact is to ask where the person's children attend school. Whether it's kindergarten or college, discussing a child's school is an easy conversational offshoot that can reveal more affinities with the person.

Life purpose: Last but not least, ask about the person's "life purpose."

Asking people about their personal passions is another way to find common ground and create a foundation for a business relationship. Many people are truly passionate about their favorite charity, brilliant children, or favorite football team. If you can get them talking about their one true passion, you've forged a meaningful and memorable connection that builds trust and likeability.

I can tell you from experience how paying the B-I-L-L can pay off. While attending a local networking event, I struck up a conversation with "Max" (not his real name) who owns a small marketing company. I started steering our conversation through the steps of the B-I-L-L and discovered quickly that his life purpose was focused on the Boy Scouts of America organization and helping boys grow into responsible and respectful young men. Within minutes of "hello," Max delivered a soliloquy regarding the state of our children in this country and how they need to get back to nature and toughen up. We agreed that kids need more real-world experience and less "phone and video game" time.

During our exchange, I learned that Max spends every opportunity to take various local Boy Scout troops into local forest preserves to improve their self-preservation skills and teach them independence. In this case, it was clear that the Boy Scouts of America and character building in children was more than a hobby or casual interest to Max; it was his life purpose. He believed that, without developing our youth, the world would cease to function in 15 or 20 years. The relationship we started that day has become an ongoing dialogue that's lasted for years. During the time we have done business together, I've continued to be impressed with his commitment to his cause. (7-A)

Sample Questions to pay the B-I-L-L

B

Business

- How did you get started in your business?
- What do you love about your business?
- What are some of the challenges you face in your industry?

I

Interests

- When you're not busy working, what do you do for fun?
- I know you're into traveling to exotic places, where was your favorite place/experience?

L

Loved Ones

- What are your kids ages?
- What are teenagers into these days?

L

Life Purpose

- I saw that you're involved in the _____ charity. Tell me more about the cause?
- I hear you're quite the golfer. Bob said you've played golf in over 20 different countries…

7-A

The idea behind "paying the B-I-L-L" is to get to a more personal level with the new contact. Forget about yourself and your services for a short time and focus instead on asking great questions and really tuning in to the answers. The person who shares some personal information with you may become a new best friend, strategic partner, or future client. At your next networking event, be sure to pay the B-I-L-L.

CHAPTER SEVEN TAKEAWAYS

- Be inquisitive and pay the B-I-L-L:
- Understanding people better by listening to their stories is the best way to build new relationships. People like us when we listen, understand, and are empathetic. We don't need to talk a lot to be well regarded.
- Building rapport is done through a dialogue that doesn't focus on you or your services but features the individual you're talking with.
- Start by asking questions. Use the B-I-L-L to remember topics for discussion.
- Dig deeper with follow-up questions that allow you an insider's look at your new contact's life.

Networking Note

"During your initial one-on-one meeting with a contact, you should ascertain the business needs of the individual or his or her company. The key to success is being proactive subsequent to a personal encounter by identifying opportunities to address the individual's needs without being engaged as counsel."

—GARY LEVENSTEIN, NIXON PEABODY LLP

8

Being a "True Giver" when Networking

Over the past 10 – 15 years there has been a dramatic increase in the number of people actively focusing on networking. Increasing competition, along with more widespread attention on building a strong network, is encouraging businesspeople to flock to networking functions in droves. This is as true for the legal profession as for any other. However, it can be an especially difficult challenge for an attorney to simultaneously balance a clogged office inbox with a devotion to developing a book of business.

As we've established, simply "getting out there" isn't enough in the contemporary networking scene. It's more critical now than ever before to employ a thoughtful approach to networking in order to find success. Many attorneys I work with express discomfort at the notion of networking due to fruitless past attempts, which makes the whole endeavor seem a waste of valuable time. However, applying an efficient and effective process to networking will ensure you get optimal results from your time investment.

I've categorized business networkers into three groups. In addition to identifying which group you might belong to, it's important to quickly identify which group others fit into as well. Identifying which group the person you're speaking with falls into can make or break your results.

Networker Type 1: The Taker

A "Taker" is an individual who attends numerous events and racks up an imposing collection of names and business cards as a way to push appointments and close sales. Unfortunately, these sometimes-aggressive creatures can burn enough people that word "gets around" and ultimately helps to dissolve their reputations. You may even start to observe people physically positioning themselves away from a Taker at consecutive events. Although avoidance seems an appropriate strategy, the Taker should not be dismissed outright. For some people, simply obtaining new sales (however generated) is and always will be their focus.

Perhaps a compassionate view toward seemingly aggressive Takers is the best way to view them. After all, many entrepreneurs require sales quotas of their employees to retain their jobs as a strategy to keep the business viable. Some Takers simply haven't been taught the art of networking, or are confused on how best to to utilize networking in order to achieve long-term results.

That being said, if you can detect a Taker early on at an event, try to avoid the next step: the one-on-one meeting. This important meeting is where you schedule a time to meet for coffee or lunch after the initial networking event where you met with a potential business connection. If you find yourself inadvertently ensnared in a meeting with a

Taker, this meeting can make for a rough few hours consisting of a sales pitch for the Taker's product or service, whether you have a need for it or not. It could also turn into a "name grab" by the new acquaintance for the names of your contacts so that he or she can make a sales pitch to them.

Whatever the case, identifying and avoiding a Taker at an event or by phone before committing to a coffee meeting can save you time and emotional energy. Feel free to thank the person for his or her time and express appreciation for the invitation, but tell the "wannabe" contact directly that you're not available and/or not interested in his or her product or service. It's perfectly acceptable to say you're happy with your current vendor. The most important thing to remember when dealing with a Taker is to use whichever response best fits your situation, get it said, and move on as quickly as possible. Your ability to identify a Taker and then to remove yourself and focus on more promising prospects is a critical component of effective networking.

Networker Type 2: The Apparent Giver

The Apparent Giver is the most common networker type. Apparent Givers are those people who, sometime during their careers, have heard and taken very much to heart the concept that "givers gain" or "give to get" as a mantra relating to networking. They believe they understand how to network and think of themselves as major players in the networking game, but often they miss the boat on the important component of follow-through.

Where Apparent Givers stumble is in failing to execute the promises they've made to new contacts in an effort to gain their trust. While an Apparent Giver may actually have altruistic intentions in the beginning, promises are worthless if the networker doesn't follow up and carry out the pledge made to the new contact. Some Apparent Givers become too distracted by other commitments and simply forget to act on their earlier promises. Some with less philanthropic motives may drop the ball when they realize the new contact may not be able to immediately reciprocate. For most people in this age of information overload, if something isn't scheduled and written down, it probably won't happen.

The most obvious downside to turning into an Apparent Giver is that failure to follow through will tarnish your reputation if you come to be viewed as someone who doesn't act on a pledge to a new contact. On the receiving end of the networking exchange, Apparent Givers present a distraction from your ultimate goal of disqualifying this contact type as a potential strategic partner due to empty promises.

When I meet an Apparent Giver, I always perform a small test. I ask this potential Apparent Giver to make an introduction for me to a third party to observe the person's follow-through. If the Apparent Giver seems to stumble on the action portion of the equation, I may step in and try to help the person out with a reminder e-mail or phone call to discuss progress on the referral that was offered. After that, if my prompts don't bear fruit, I begin to seriously question my new contact's ability to become a referral source for me. This low-commitment testing process provides me with an opportunity to gauge the new contact's mettle in terms of living up to promises before spending time on someone who's unable to be an active part of my network due to inertia. The same approach can work for you.

Networker Type 3: The True Giver

The ultimate networking aspiration is to become a True Giver and to seek to interact with others of this type. True Givers understand the "big picture" when it comes to networking. This networker's mantra is "I'll give selflessly, regardless of what's in it for me personally."

As a True Giver, I can tell you that giving selflessly to everyone you meet is a fulfilling way of life in and of itself. The amount of good karma I've stockpiled over the years of true giving is impressive, if I do say so myself. I've built a mega network 15,000 people deep with a stellar reputation as a dependable person.

The downside of being a True Giver comes down to a math problem. When I started networking many years ago, I attended three or four networking events each week. Depending on the type of event, I'd meet from 3 to 20 new people at each event. Early on, I filled up my calendar with anyone, including C-classified contacts (see Chapter 5), who'd meet with me. There were days I'd go to five coffee meetings back-to-back.

As a newbie True Giver, I felt that in order to succeed at networking on a high level, I had to help each and every person I met for a cup of joe. However, even if I met for only 3 coffees each day, in a month of 20 working days that would have amounted to 60 individuals that I was trying to assist with referrals — and I was making as many as 3 connections for each person I met for coffee. When I make a referral, it's typically a call on the contact's behalf for optimal results, which could take three minutes, minimum. All this adds up to 540 minutes of referral time, give or take, each month. That's 9 hours each month just making phone calls, in addition to the time spent meeting with the contacts in the first place — which is untenable, even for the most committed True Giver. (8-A)

As a busy attorney, you're probably reading this and shaking your head in disbelief due to not just the sheer number of meetings, but the astonishing amount of time I'd spend introducing contacts to each other. Even if you had only five short coffee meetings in a month, it might be problematic to then make one quality introduction for each. That's why being a True Giver has to be balanced with a deliberate process.

What type of networker are you?

Score yourself on a 1-5 scale (1 being terrible and 5 being top-notch)

When at a networking event, you focus 100% on the person who is speaking to you.	(1, 2, 3, 4, 5)
When at a networking event, you ask questions to identify how you can help someone else.	(1, 2, 3, 4, 5)
When at a coffee meeting, you identify one or two ways you can help or add value for the other person.	(1, 2, 3, 4, 5)
After meeting with someone, you immediately make the introductions you had suggested.	(1, 2, 3, 4, 5)
You regularly follow-up to ensure that connections were made and your new friend is happy.	(1, 2, 3, 4, 5)

Rate yourself:

5-10 = possible taker | 11-17= possible apparent giver | 18-25= possible real giver (nice work!)

8-A

First and foremost, remember that you don't have to meet with everyone you encounter at a networking event, as we've already established. By using the system outlined in Chapter 5 to qualify the best people for you to endeavor to meet and possibly refer to another connection, you'll focus in on quality connections.

Second, don't feel obligated to promise referrals for every person you meet. Not everyone is worthy of your "endorsement" by way of an introduction to another one of the contacts you've nurtured. It's fairly easy to disqualify Takers and industry nonexperts as people not to make pledges to or introduce to others.

Finally, while of course the Golden Rule tells us we should be nice to everyone, you should focus your networking energy on helping those people you identify as True Givers and those who appear to have the ability to be a strategic partner over the long haul.

One major key to successful networking is to qualify people *as you go*. This is critical because, from a temporal standpoint, you should be following up as close in time to the networking event as possible. Because all networkers are not created equal, you should make sure they're tested and then tested again. You'll learn more about your new contact with each interaction. For example, after meeting someone for coffee and rating her as an A, I may try to make one or two introductions for her. Along the way, I watch her reaction and reciprocation. While I don't necessarily expect "tit for tat," if there isn't some level of reciprocity, I know I've met someone who's probably not a True Giver, which informs my interactions surrounding this person going forward.

While other networking resources might suggest that being a True Giver requires never asking the "return on investment" question, I posit that effective networking requires informed, judicious giving of your time and connections to the right people for the right reasons. After all, there just aren't enough hours in the day to run around doing good deeds for every person who crosses our paths.

On another note, I may meet a contact I rate as a C and try to make one small connection for him or her or provide some sound advice if asked. I don't necessarily expect much from a C in return, but this is where the "networking karma" kicks in. My father always said, "If you can't make a sale, make a friend." This is a surefire way to build up a following of people who like you and might think about referring you down the road.

CHAPTER EIGHT TAKEAWAYS

- Being a True Giver is ideal, but it isn't natural for many people. The key is to the connect with the right people for the right reasons.
- It's okay to walk away from Takers and Apparent Givers. The return on investment with these two groups will rarely be fruitful.
- We all have the ability to be a True Giver. If you can unleash it with intelligence, it could be the most rewarding business activity in which you engage.
- For most people, becoming a True Giver is a learned skill. Like any other skill, it needs to be used, practiced, and improved on for real results to occur.

Networking Note

"*Effective rainmakers consistently provide their most trusted relationships with what they need, whether it be legal services, key introductions, ideas, industry information, or referrals. Networking and building a following allows you to provide more value in the relationships that you are developing. It enables you to give far more than quality legal services, which are a given.*"

—JEFFREY STAHL, STAHL COWEN CROWLEY ADDIS LLC

9

Organizing and Controlling One-on-One Meetings for Better Results

M any of the attorneys I speak with loathe the entire concept of networking. For some, the "salesy" connotation associated with it is troubling. For others, it's the time it takes away from billing hours that's distasteful. The belief that any and all networking activities will help you grow your practice is a misnomer. The reality is that networking can be a massive drain on your time if not done effectively.

To some degree, networking is, in essence, a numbers game. Your odds improve by attending the right events frequented by the right people and employing the right approach. The key to improving your networking odds is to better prepare and execute your plan in advance, and learn from your mistakes.

After attending over 1,100 events and personally meeting over 6,000 people, I've found it to be most important to be time savvy time during one-on-one meetings you set with contacts. How you conduct yourself in a one-on-one meeting can make the difference between success and failure in effectively networking your practice.

As with the other aspects of networking, a methodical approach to one-on-one meetings will significantly increase your success rate from attending events and conferences. Note that the following strategies are specific to meeting someone new for the purposes of a strategic partnership. While there are elements that can be used with an old friend or new potential client, the focus of this chapter is to qualify new acquaintances for strategic partnership purposes.

First Things First: Carefully Qualify Your Prospects Prior to the One-on-One Meeting

The first thing to remember is that qualifying a new potential strategic partner after an event is a critical aspect of networking. This isn't to say that meeting one-on-one with everyone you speak with isn't an option. However, as we've established, it's just not the most effective way to go. Asking some good questions when meeting someone new is a good way to learn to qualify (or disqualify) the person as someone with whom you should invest your networking time. Revealing questions to ask include:

- "How long have you been in business?"
- "What do you look for in a strategic partner for your business?"
- "What can you tell me about your networking activities and the types of people you usually help?"
- "Whom do you currently partner with to get referrals?"
- "What should I be listening for in a good referral for you?"

The idea behind asking these questions is to gain an understanding of your contact's ability to act as a True Giver and possibly a strategic partner for you. If you find that the individual is "newer" to the business game, is clearly out only for himself or herself, or already has an established partner in your industry, you may not want to invest much time, if any, connecting further with this individual.

Since time is one of the most valued assets in business, networkers must be careful about those they choose to actually meet. I always recommend a follow-up call prior to meeting in order to requalify a new potential strategic partner. I've saved myself a great deal of time on many occasions by slowing things down and not scheduling a face-to-face meeting until after I've had a 10 – 15 minute telephone conversation with my new acquaintance first.

Treat One-on-One Meetings as You Would Any Professional Meeting and Set an Agenda

Once a contact has been qualified, in certain instances it will make sense to set up a one-on-one networking meeting. In addition to finding a quiet place to meet, we want to really set the table to ensure success. As with any other professional meeting, creating and following an agenda is a basis for reaching a professional connection beyond a short conversation at a crowded event.

Because the person you're meeting with is essentially a stranger, you need to take control of the meeting from the beginning in order to ensure that both parties have a successful outcome. Without the structure of an agenda, a first meeting can go in any number of directions. In the past, these meetings have subjected me to two-hour sales pitches and a photo review of a person's family Disney trip. As you can imagine, I found this to be a complete waste of time. By taking a few minutes to establish an agenda or game plan, you not only take control of the meeting but retain the ability to cut it short if the direction becomes unfruitful.

Just before you launch into your meeting agenda, it's always a good idea to take a little time to build some rapport with your contact to warm up the exchange. Early in the one-on-one meeting is the opportune time to "pay the B-I-L-L" as discussed in Chapter 7. Don't forget that uncovering and then discussing natural affinities always sets a positive tone at the beginning of a networking meeting.

After exchanging pleasantries, suggest to your contact that you work through the following game plan during this networking one-on-one.

Step 1: Ask permission to set an agenda or game plan for the meeting.

Make sure you communicate that you're not forcing your agenda on the other person. To do this, couch it terms of asking that person's permission to establish a framework for the meeting that works for both parties. If this is uncomfortable, you can use the following statement: "I really appreciate you taking the time to meet with me today. In order to make the most of our time together, I thought it would make sense to set up a little game plan for our meeting this morning. Is that okay with you?" This approach is a foolproof way to gain buy in from your contact. After all, your contact is not likely to respond that he or she would prefer to waste the meeting time. (Incidentally, if that should happen, there's your cue to run for the hills.) Once buy-in occurs, and it surely will, you should move to actually setting the agenda.

Step 2: Establish or reconfirm the time limit for your meeting.

The last thing you or your contact wants is to be stuck in a directionless meeting with someone. By establishing a time limit, you're protecting your valuable time. Confirm the timeline by reminding your contact that you agreed to set aside a specific amount of time in advance. Again, if you're uncomfortable, you can use this simple phrasing: "We'd agreed on the phone to meet for an hour. We have 50 minutes left; are you still good with that?" I also make a point to shut my phone off in front of my contact, as a cue to him or her to do the same. A ringing cell phone in the middle of a meeting is rude and disruptive to the networking process. Please lead the charge in this regard and turn off your cell phone first.

If the meeting is creeping past the time limit and you've determined that it's not going well, feel free to tell your contact that you have another meeting scheduled and have to run. The fact that you set the hour time limit allows you to do this without feeling that you're being rude or dismissive to your contact. Bear in mind that you both agreed in advance to the specific time frame, so don't feel guilty about sticking to it.

Step 3: Ask for the contact's agreement that the purpose is to see if there's a "fit."

Isn't that what this is all about anyway? We're looking for a win-win relationship and need to establish a "fit" as the goal for our meeting. This part is simple; you just say, "From my perspective, the purpose of us meeting today is for us to determine if there's a 'fit' to work together. Does that sound good to you?" In my experience, people respond well to the word "fit."

On the other hand, if the meeting isn't going well and you realize that there's not a fit, don't hesitate to speak up and gain the contact's agreement to move on and not work together. Remember, not everyone will be a fit for you, and that's okay. If prospects for a mutually beneficial connection aren't looking good, you might say, "Earlier in our meeting we agreed that the purpose was to see if there was a fit to work together. Based on our conversation so far, it doesn't appear there is a good fit." Take another 30 seconds to explain why there might not be a good fit and help the contact understand. If you're completely uncomfortable bringing this up to someone, just let the meeting run its course over the hour and simply move on.

Step 4: Establish clear expectations for both parties.

Vocalizing the expectations each of you has for the meeting is important to ensure balance during the meeting between talking and listening. Both components are important for both parties to learn about each other's business and potential needs. By addressing this issue directly, you're equalizing the discussion and warding off the frustration that ensues when one person monopolizes the conversation, with the "talker" later wanting another meeting because he or she learned nothing about you or your practice.

The best way to state this, if you're unsure, is to say, "I was hoping that you could spend about 15 minutes telling me more about your business, how you help people, and the types of people you're looking to meet. Then I can do the same once you're done. How does that sound to you?"

Spelling out the parameters sets the stage to keep the conversation on track and communicates a goal of efficiently using the limited time you have for the one-on-one meeting. As with your request to set an agenda, phrasing this sentiment as a question should allow you to feel free to step in if the contact starts off on a tangent and prompt him or her to keep on track. You can always politely interrupt someone who's dominating the conversation to remind the person of the time frame so you can reach the mutually agreed on goal to learn both sides of the story before time runs out.

Step 5: Articulate a positive outcome for both parties.

The final step in the agenda-setting process is the most important of all. This is the confirmation of a commitment to mutually help one another in some small way if there should be a fit. A good way to introduce this topic is to state, "At the end of our meeting, if we see that there's a clear fit for us to help one another, I'd suggest we try to take a small step forward together, such as making an easy connection for one another or inviting one another to attend an upcoming event. How do you feel about that?"

The reason this is so effective is because it advances and emphasizes the quid pro quo of the ultimate goal in meeting: connections. Think about what your new contact might be seeking from you. Most likely it's the same thing you're after: a positive connection that benefits both parties. By agreeing to start small, you're not investing too much of yourself and not receiving so much that you might walk away with a sense of obligation to the contact. The goal of the "baby step" is to test the connection without over- or under-committing, much like tasting a wine before buying an entire bottle.

For some attorneys, there may be a level of discomfort with this "formulaic" approach. If that's the case, you're not alone. I've heard, "I can't see myself saying that," or "This sounds too formal for me." If this is the case, you should adjust the sentiment to fit your natural, comfortable speaking pattern. If you have trouble with this, try out the phrasing provided and see what happens.

I've worked with hundreds of attorneys in learning to set an agenda for the one-on-one networking meeting, and then following a prescribed approach, and even those who expressed reluctance end up finding great success using it. As you can see, there's nothing threatening about setting an agenda. Everything is permission-based and agreed to by both parties. By taking control of your networking meetings, everyone can get something of value from the time they've invested. (9-A)

Why do we need to set up a game plan or agenda for our networking coffee meetings?

Without an agenda

The meeting is all over the place. The meeting can last 30 minutes or 3 hours!

The other person wants to sell you "things."

The other person talks for 75 minutes without breathing.

There is no next step or introductions committed to.

With an agenda

The meeting is focused and controlled by you.

The meeting is limited to 60 minutes (unless you want it to last longer).

The meeting is set up to see how we may help one another.

You split up the talk time to ensure both parties are heard.

A quid pro quo outcome is agree to up front.

9-A

In some cases, the benefit might be in finding out that there's no "fit" between you and the contact. If that's the case, simply move this person to the "not a good fit" category. Every time you disqualify someone who's not a good fit for you, you're thinning out the herd and keeping your network focused on the best partners for you. No one really wants to continue to spend time with someone who's not a good fit as a strategic partner. Once the agenda is set, you're ready to execute on a successful one-on-one meeting with your new friend.

In order to run the one-on-one meeting effectively, follow this approach:

1. Put the other person first.

Ask your contact to start explaining his or her business to you. Remember, the contact should get the first 15 minutes of the conversation to speak. By asking the contact to go first, you might uncover information that could change how you present your service offerings.

For example, assume you're an estate planning attorney meeting with a financial planner who focuses on high-net-worth individuals with estates over $5 million. When it's your turn to speak and share your work, it might make sense to avoid mentioning that you're happy working with just about anyone on an estate plan. You could modify your extended infomercial to describe the larger and more complex estates that you've worked on and prefer. This will help you better match your skills with the financial planner's client base.

2. Be prepared with questions that might help qualify the contact as a strategic partner or a prospective client.

I've had many meetings that started out as a potential strategic partner meeting, but soon turned into a prospective client meeting due to my questions or how I presented my service offerings. There are also questions that may uncover the types of leads the contact has in his or her network that might be fruitful connections for you, including:

- "With whom do you network to find new business?"
- "Where do you find you get the best networking results?"
- "What are some of the networking methods you use to maximize the value of your business?"
- "What referral sources are best for you?"
- "Who are some of your best strategic partners?"
- "What industries or 'verticals' (groups of people within a specific industry) do you serve?"
- "What size companies do you typically work with?"
- "Can you describe your clients?"
- "What makes you or your company unique?"
- "Who's your competition?"
- "What are some of the challenges your company faces every day?"
- "How does the economy affect your business?"
- "What are your expectations from your best strategic partners?"
- "Where do you see yourself and your company in five years?"
- "Can you tell me why you love what you do?"
- "How often do you interact with GCs, CEOs, and CFOs?"

While there are hundreds of questions you can ask, try to zero in on three to five that make sense for you and the person you're meeting with. Your ability to listen, ask questions, and dig deeper will dramatically improve your success in these networking meetings.

Keep your ears peeled for talking points that might turn your networking meeting into a prospective client meeting. If you believe you're going into a networking meeting with a person who might also be a good client for you, be sure to ask questions that uncover certain needs or pain points. For example, let's say that you're a litigator and you're networking over coffee with a general counsel you met at a conference. Be sure to ask questions like:

- "I see that you've been with ABC Corp. for a year. Would you tell me more about how you became their GC?"
- "How many divisions does your company have?"
- "What are some of the challenges that your company faces every day?"
- "How many people are in your department, and what's your specific role?"
- "What kind of legal work do you typically outsource?"
- "What qualities do you seek in a litigation firm?"

While you're not coming straight out and directly asking the contact for his or her business, you're learning more about the opportunity in front of you and setting the stage for a discussion about your potential to work with the person and/or his or her business. If you can uncover a few issues your contact is currently facing or expects to have in the future, there may be an opening for you to request the business.

In some instances, there may be little to no opportunity for new business. You might have to be patient with this contact. With some contacts, it can take years to develop the type of trust and relationship that makes the contact comfortable working with you. Sometimes being in the "number two" position pays off, when the client's current business relationship falls away. You'll want to be there and come to your contact's mind when someone else drops the ball. Of course, another option is to simply disqualify the contact as a potential resource for you and move on. Again, moving someone to the "no" category can be empowering, freeing up your precious networking time to focus on contacts who may actually work with you.

CHAPTER NINE TAKEAWAYS

- Get comfortable with a systematic approach to the one-on-one networking meeting. If the idea of using an agenda to guide a one-on-one meeting with a new contact feels awkward to you, follow these tips to become more comfortable with the approach:

- Use my language. While you can make small changes to the script to fit your personal style, initially you should avoid straying too far from my words and the specific steps in the approach outlined in this book. Improvisation can lead to missteps and take away the effectiveness of the approach.

- Use the agenda approach to keep the meeting on track. Setting an agenda for a networking meeting will almost always result in a better outcome. It can save you time and help you identify fruitful opportunities.

- Remember that this meeting can help disqualify a contact as well. Keep your radar up for statements and behavior that turn you off. Ask yourself if you like the person. Take note of whether he or she is listening to you and asking you "smart" questions. Notice whether the person offers up a name or blows you off with vague promises.
- Ask pointed questions to uncover opportunities to make a good strategic partner or prospective client.
- Remember to get the contact talking first. Next, make sure you ask relevant and revealing questions. Third, dig deeper to see if the contact has a legal need or pain that you might be able to help solve. Finally, learn all you can to understand whether this person can really refer you and you him or her.

Networking Note

"Job one of a good networker is learning about another person's goal in some area of his or her life and then helping the person move closer to accomplishing it."

—LANE MOYER, VEDDER PRICE

10

Turning Referrals into Quality Introductions

One of the most challenging parts of networking is asking for quality introductions. Unfortunately, for many attorneys this isn't something that comes naturally; it's not only uncomfortable, but downright terrifying. Even more daunting, the referrals we *do* ask for are rarely qualified to do business with us at all.

Referrals vs. Quality Introductions

So what's the difference between a referral and a quality introduction? A referral is a lead or potential contact, typically including the individual's name and phone number, passed on to you by a strategic partner. Unfortunately, many times this results in a glorified "cold call," requiring you to chase after the person. In addition to not knowing if the prospective client is even interested in your legal services, no effort has been made to ensure your success with this new connection.

In a quality introduction, on the other hand, your strategic partner not only gives you the contact information but verbally contacts and prequalifies the prospective client, providing positive affirmations about how you met, why he or she believes your services are of value, and most important how you may help solve a problem for the prospect. This preliminary phone call made on your behalf ensures that the prospect will actually be receptive to your call.

Barriers to Obtaining Quality Introductions

Typically, there are three main barriers that must be overcome to obtain quality introductions. They include:

Head trash. You may have fear regarding the perception of asking for an introduction. The thought that you might come across as pandering, salesy, or even a beggar will not help you in obtaining introductions.

Lack of the proper approach. If you have no set process for approaching strategic partners to comfortably obtain quality introductions, and since the idea of "winging it" and possibly failing is scary, it's easy to decide it's better not to try at all.

Not having the proper language. Without the right language to ask your strategic partners for quality introductions, you might come across as pushy or aggressive. The right words can make all the difference.

To be successful in coaching your networking partners to make quality introductions on your behalf, you must overcome any negative feelings you have about asking for things and make the situation more comfortable for both parties by using a solid process and the appropriate language.

Taking Out the "Head Trash"

"Head trash" is the reservations, fears, and negative past experiences that keep us from thinking and acting clearly to achieve the results we desire.

For example, if you aren't currently comfortable being asked for a referral from a referral partner, chances are you won't feel comfortable asking for one yourself. Another important factor in removing "head trash" is your belief. You must truly believe that you're the best and most qualified individual in your industry and that everyone is better off working with you rather than anyone else.

Using the Proper Approach and Language

To overcome your fears and get real results in working with your strategic partners, follow these simple steps:

Step 1: Remember to find a quiet place to meet and begin building rapport.

As mentioned in Chapter 9, be sure to set an agenda for the meeting. Ask probing questions to identify who the partner knows and where you can solve problems for them. When it's your turn to speak, use your infomercial (see Chapter 4), and speak to the successes you've had in your area of the law. Tell stories and give specific examples that will show your value to your strategic partner's best connections. This will help to get the partner thinking about his or her network and who you might be a good fit for you to meet or help.

Step 2: At some point near the end of the meeting, bring up the connections you can share with one another.

You could say, "I know when we spoke earlier that we were going to try to make one small connection for one another. I believe I have a good contact for you. I'm just curious whether there's anyone you had in mind for me to speak with?" By bringing up the possible connections, you can take ten minutes or so to work through them to see which possible contacts make sense to pursue.

Step 3: Get a name from your strategic partner while he or she is still with you.

The reason this is so important is because once the partner says, "Sure thing; I'll get back to you with some names in a few weeks," and leaves, it's probably over. The sad truth is that your partner will probably get busy after returning to his or her office, and the small commitment that you asked for may never cross his or her mind again. You must strike while the iron is hot and ask for a specific name right there and then. Try saying one of the following:

- "Who do you know who would work really well with me?"
- "I know you work with a lot of manufacturers. Who are some of your closest relationships?"
- "Who are some of your key vendors that might be open to an introduction?"

- "I know you're heavily involved in your charity. Who are some of the board members who have their own business?"
- "When you play golf at your club, who are some of the people you play with?"

By ferreting out a specific group, you have a greater chance of getting a particular name of someone willing to meet you. Sometimes you have to work to open two or three doors within someone's network to obtain the right name for you. Another important point to remember is that it's okay to nicely reject an introduction if it isn't right for you. As a sales coach, people are always trying to introduce me to others who are in my industry, but in my world there's little to no value in meeting people with similar service offerings. The point here is to be selective. Don't just say "yes" because someone mentions a name. It's okay to thank your strategic partner and continue working to find someone who's a better fit.

Step 4: Move referrals to quality introductions by asking your strategic partner to make a personal call on your behalf to help ensure the introduction will actually occur.

For example, once a solid name is brought up and agreed on, say, "Would you do me a personal favor? Please call your friend and give him a little background on how we met and why you believe he should speak with me. Then see if he's open to and will accept my call."

In some cases, you may actually want to role-play the conversation with your partner to ensure he or she knows how to handle the introduction properly. By moving the referral to a quality introduction, your chances of obtaining a meeting go way up.

Step 5: Follow through.

Setting specific next steps with your strategic partner will also help to ensure everything comes together. If he or she has committed to make the introduction on your behalf, be sure to set a time frame for that to happen.

You could say, "Would you be able to call your friend by the end of the week? And once you've done so, would you send an e-mail to both of us so we have each other's contact information?"

Sometimes with someone whom I know has poor follow-up skills I'll ask, "I know how busy you get. If I don't hear from you in a week, what's the best way for me to check in with you on this?" This approach gives me permission to gently remind my partner that he or she dropped the ball. Setting up a specific next step or time frame will reduce the risk of your partner holding off on making the call for you. (10-A)

Referral versus a Quality Introduction
Which one is better for everyone involved?

Referral

Only a name and number are provided.

The prospect is too busy to "deal" with you.

When you call, the referral is blindsided.

Your new referral partner does very little.

What's the end result of a poorly set up referral? It could be a three-way loser!

- The prospect never responds, so you lose.
- The referral partner is bothered that the referral didn't connect.
- The prospect loses because she never gets to meet you AND if she does eventually, there might be some guilt in their initial reluctance to call you back.

Quality Introduction

A call is made on your behalf to qualify the referral as someone who may need your services.

The prospect is waiting for you to reach out and open to a dialogue.

Your call is welcomed, due to the introduction previously made.

Your referral partner is "tested" to see how influential she really is to help you get in the door.

10-A

Once you have a name and firm commitment from your partner to make a quality introduction, you'll be more inclined to step up and provide a name or two for him or her. This reciprocation is the cornerstone of networking. By taking control of the process, you're ensuring a much better outcome than might happen by "winging it."

By practicing these steps and making them your own, you'll take a potentially uncomfortable situation and make it a win-win. Though this isn't easy, once you've done it two or three times, you'll become a pro at getting quality introductions on a regular basis. It's possible that you might not have to do much else to keep your pipeline filled month after month.

CHAPTER TEN TAKEAWAYS

- Get rid of the "head trash" by believing that you're the best at helping others. People will like you and want to help you as long as it's reciprocal. You're not asking for something that you're not willing to give.
- Help upgrade the referral into a quality introduction by preparing your strategic partner to introduce you through the use of a proper approach and proper language.

Networking Note

"When deciding how to spend my networking time, I focus on the personal qualities and habits of my networking partners, rather than their occupations. It is more important to have networking partners who 'get it' — who are talented networkers — regardless of their occupation or environment. And if there is someone who 'gets it' whose work also brings them in contact with my potential clients all the time, that's a home run."

— NEIL DISHMAN, JACKSON LEWIS P.C.

11

Developing the Best Strategic Partners

Why do we network? For most of us, it's because we believe that we'll find new business at the events we attend. The reality is that very little business will be found at these events, especially if you sell into the middle or large markets

So what *should* we be looking for at these events? Strategic partners!

A good strategic partner is someone who'll introduce you to the prospective clients that you're looking to meet. For example, a large part of my business is selling into the legal market. Therefore, it makes a lot of sense for me to develop strategic partnerships with others who sell into the legal market as well.

While that may seem simple, the majority of business development professionals aren't doing this at a high enough level. I see their frustration grow as they continue to network more and more, having little to show at the end of the day. In my experience, the best strategic partners are people who share the same qualities and values that you have.

A few years ago, one of my brightest clients came up with a terrific acronym that defines the qualities we should all be looking for in a solid strategic partner. It's T-L-E-N-D, which stands for "trust," "like," "expert," "network," and "decision-maker."

Trust: Though the trustworthiness of a potential strategic partner is difficult to uncover at an event or during an initial one-hour networking meeting, try to give your prospective partner a few tasks to work on for you. This will help you to better understand his or her ability to follow up and stand behind commitments made to you. Multiple missed calls or rescheduled appointments with you should be warning signs that this person may not follow through very well. Breaking commitments to others is the same as breaking someone's trust.

Like: In order to create a long-term and productive relationship with another business professional, it's imperative that you actually like one another. Finding someone that you could be friends with will help to ensure that a long-term sustainable relationship can exist. In many cases, your ability to find areas of common ground will help you through this process. Ask yourself if this is someone you'd want to bring home for dinner. We need to like someone to stay engaged long term as a strategic partner.

Expert: One of the worst feelings you can have is referring a phony or incompetent person to one of your friends or clients. Having a clear understanding of someone's true skill sets and ability to follow through will help you in determining if he or she is actually referable. Look for online recommendations, testimonials, and an overall track record of success with his or her clients. Ask questions to better understand the person's background and experience in the field. Who has he or she worked with? What does he or she know about his or her subject? How long has he or she been in the business? If an individual can't validate his or her skills and accomplishments, it might be a warning sign for you to move on.

Network: As you can imagine, it's hard to obtain referrals if your new contact doesn't know anyone. Finding a new strategic partner who's "wired in" to the marketplace can make or break your ability to obtain the referrals you're looking for. Though the average person statistically has over 250 people in his or her immediate network, finding someone with high-level connections may fast-track your success in developing strong strategic partners.

While I tend to shy away from folks with small networks, remember that it only takes one good connection to help you obtain a new client. Of all the qualifiers, this is the one I look past most often. In some cases, I take a call or a meeting with someone starting out. It's easy to invite such an individual to an event I'm holding or introduce him or her to someone I know. These are the karma points that come back to you.

Decision-maker: While it's not imperative to partner with CEOs, presidents, and general counsel, it doesn't hurt to network with high-level executives when you can. In my experience, most executives are connected with other executives, which is good reason to nurture these relationships. These connections also help when you're looking to make referrals to your strategic partners. Remember, the other half of networking is connecting your strategic partners with high-level folks. The more you know, the stronger you become as someone else's strategic partner. (11-A)

Take the TLEND Challenge

Take a look at your network and determine how many strategic partners you really have? How many would pass the TLEND challenge?

Trust: When a strategic partner commits something to you, does he consistently follow through?

Like: Do you enjoy spending time and working along side your strategic partner?

Expert: Can your strategic partner handle all questions related to his field and make you look great?

Network: Does your strategic partner have a large network of contacts that are relevant to your practice?

Decision Maker: Is your strategic partner a high-level player in his industry?

If you run your top ten strategic partners through this challenge, you might find:
- A strategic partner that needs to be replaced.
- A strategic partner that needs to be further cultivated (more time with him).
- A strategic partner that needs to be given more value from you (i.e. Provide more quality introductions for him.)

11-A

CHAPTER ELEVEN TAKEAWAYS

- Remember the acronym T-L-E-N-D when you're attending events or meeting people one-on-one and use it to qualify people so you can invest your time wisely.

- Trust, likeability, and expertise are critical elements to qualifying. If you're a networker, you know how bad it feels to make a terrible introduction. No one wins, and it has the potential to devastate a relationship.

Networking Note

"Networking is a lifelong process, not a one-night event. It's about being savvy, helpful, and most of all present. Stay in the mind of those you want to serve."

—GREGORY BRAUN, BRAUN & RICH

12

Building Your Networking "Dream Team"

Effective networking isn't always about attending every event and meeting with everyone you can. It's really about focusing your efforts the right way, with the right people. As you continue to meet and qualify people, try to select the best "key players" and test them out to make sure they're a good fit for you and your business goals. Bring them up slowly and with care. If you've found the right people, it can mean the difference between success and failure in building your legal practice.

Scouting the Field for Champions

When thinking about developing the strongest strategic partnerships, imagine yourself as a baseball scout searching for winning players for a major league ball club. You'd probably research the areas where the best ball players have traditionally been found. Then you'd go to these key areas and watch the players play. While there, you'd analyze their skills, abilities, and potential. What are they willing to do to be the best at the game and win championships? How do they get along with their teammates?

How do they throw, run, hit, and catch? Are they consistent in their performance game after game? How do they handle pressure?

After observing and speaking to one terrific player, you decide to invite him or her to play ball for you. Does this new player go right to the starting lineup of your major league team? Of course not! A major league team would never replace a highly paid professional with an unproven entity without bringing the rookie up the right way. It would start the individual out on the farm team or minor league squad to see how he or she does. Only after the individual shows a consistent performance over time would the team even consider moving him or her up to the big league.

So how does this relate to networking?

When trying to develop the best strategic partners, try to follow the same general principles as a baseball scout. Always have your antenna up when looking for new partnerships at the events you attend. Then meet one-on-one with the individuals who show the most potential and discuss how you can help each other. Keep in mind that you've just met these people and shouldn't put them on your strategic partner dream team just yet.

Try each individual out first over the next month or two, and then ask yourself the following questions:

- Does this person truly understand the meaning of networking?
- What's the size and connectivity of his or her network?

- Is this person the best at what he or she does, and can the person back up what he or she says?
- How's this person doing at referring you as you refer him or her?
- Are the introductions qualified or unqualified?
- Does this person follow up on the commitments being made?
- Does he or she pass the T-L-E-N-D test (see Chapter 11)?

As you work with your new partner over a period of time, observe how dependable and consistent her or she is. If someone is following through and providing value for you, it might make sense to move him or her up the ranks within your network. On the other end, if someone is falling short of expectations or is inconsistent, you might want to move him or her out of your network entirely. (12-A)

Moving a Strategic Partner up to the Majors

As a Scout for talent, here are the signs that someone should be moved up to your dream team:

- Her follow-up is second to none.
- She is always thinking about you and how to refer people your way.
- When you get together, she is always helpful and open to new ideas for quality introductions.
- She asks you for advice on the best ways to introduce you to new contacts.
- She pro-actively schedules meetings with you to discuss business development.
- She helps you to identify contacts for her, versus leaving it up to you. (using LinkedIn for example).
- You become friends and get together socially.
- She is a key element to your on-going success as an attorney.

12-A

Keeping Your Dream Team Loyal

Once you've built a team of five to ten individuals, it's important to keep your dream team happy and loyal to you. As with clients, retaining existing ones can be more valuable than developing new ones. You've already invested the time and energy, so you might as well protect your investment.

One of the biggest concerns I hear from my clients regards their ability to add enough value to the relationships they have. This usually occurs when one partner has more referrals or business to give than the other partner. As discussed in Chapter 9, a strategic partner relationship must have a win-win outcome for both parties to remain healthy. That said, value isn't only about providing new client referrals. There are a number of things you can do to add value for your strategic partners. Here are eight ways you can be effective in keeping your partners engaged and loyal to you:

- Drive direct business to your best strategic partners through your client, vendor, and personal relationships.
- Make a high-level introduction to other strategic partners in your network, which can sometimes be more valuable than providing direct business.
- Provide legal advice to your partners to help them solve a business problem.
- Be your partners' "go-to" person for anything they need, whether it's a home roofer or a CPA for business. This is much easier to do if you've been networking a while and developed a host of quality contacts.
- Invite your partners to join you at networking events, board meetings, or charity functions where you can introduce them around. Buy an extra ticket to a big event with a top-notch speaker, sit your partner at your table, and have him or her meet your clients in a natural setting.
- Start your own private networking group, and include your top strategic partners.
- Be awesome at what you do! In some cases, your strategic partners just want to refer someone who

takes care of his or her people. They're not looking for reciprocation, just excellence.

- Be social with your best strategic partners. Invite them to join you at a ball game with one of your best clients.

By using one or more of these tactics, you'll keep your best strategic partners happy and loyal to you. Sometimes we have to get creative to ensure we're adding value to the relationships we value most. Without doing for others on a consistent basis, we're opening ourselves up for disappointment when one of our partners changes teams.

CHAPTER TWELVE TAKEAWAYS

- Dream teams aren't built overnight. As in baseball, building and sustaining a successful referral powerhouse takes time, patience, and resolve.
- It isn't enough that you seem to complement each other's skill set initially; there has to be some real chemistry and mutual giving. Make the experience a quid pro quo to help grow a successful networking partnership.
- Take baby steps with people you like and believe in before rushing in too fast. Once someone has proven himself or herself as a quality referral partner, get him or her in the starting rotation and win some championships together.
- You don't need to refer business to keep strategic partners happy. There are other ways to add value. Be proactive and consistent to keep your strategic partners engaged with you.

Network Note

"As when building a skyscraper, you need to create a strong base filled with centers of influence and close allies. Then you must reinforce that base and inspect it on a regular basis. With patience and nurturing, you will develop partnerships and friendships where everyone benefits."

—THOMAS FIELD, BEERMANN PRITIKIN
MIRABELLI SWERDLOVE LLP

13

Leveraging Personal and Client Relationships

Without any question, the best way to develop new business is by leveraging your existing relationships with friends, colleagues, and most importantly clients. When given the choice to attend a networking event or have a meeting with an existing client to chat about possible introductions, I'd always choose the latter. The concern many attorneys have with this type of meeting is the underlying fear of how they'll be perceived. No one wants to come across salesy, pushy, or needy. Additionally, there's always the risk of asking for something and not getting it. Having been in business development for over 20 years, I understand how worrisome asking for business can appear to most people, particularly attorneys.

Years ago, Neale Donald Walsch explained that "FEAR is an acronym . . . for 'False Evidence Appearing Real'. " What this means is that most of the fear you may be feeling is really unwarranted to some degree. Are you swimming with sharks or walking a thousand feet up on a tightrope? The things that we should be truly afraid of don't exist as a part of our everyday lives, so we've created other fears that fit better into our world. Years ago I used to have a fear of public speaking. Just the idea of getting in front of a group made me break out in a cold sweat. However, like most things that we're afraid of, simply being prepared and doing it changed everything for me. I realized there was little to fear as long as I knew my material.

Asking for introductions or business from friends, colleagues, and clients is not that different. You must be prepared, follow a process, and use language that makes the exchange more comfortable for both parties, as noted in Chapter 10. But here are a couple of pointers specifically related to obtaining business from friends, colleagues, and clients.

Tip #1: Be sure to set up the idea of a quality introduction prior to the face-to-face meeting. No one likes surprises, so be sure to call ahead. By asking for permission to discuss possible introductions at the meeting, you're essentially adding one extra element to the agenda.

There are three solid approaches for this depending on your level of comfort with the individual and the process:

- "quid pro quo"
- "you're happy . . . should someone else be happy?"
- "I'm not comfortable asking, but . . . ."

Here's how to lay the groundwork for possible quality introductions in each:

Quid pro quo. "I know you're wired in and have lots of powerful connections. I believe I have some good ones too. Would you be open to discussing some possible introductions we could make for one another as a part of our meeting next week?"

You're happy . . . should someone else be happy? "I know you've been really happy with the work and positive results we've had together over the past few years. I was hoping we might take a few minutes near the end of our meeting next week to consider a few of your strongest connections, as they might be able to benefit from working with me as well. Is that something you'd be open to discussing briefly when we meet?"

I'm not comfortable asking, but . . . . "There's something I've been meaning to ask you, but I'm really uncomfortable with it. I'm looking to continue growing my practice and would really appreciate your help with some introductions to people you know with whom I could work. Is that something you'd be open to helping me with?"

These approaches are all permission based and logical in the way they're used. In the first option, you're offering to connect your friend, colleague, or client with people in your network, so you're not simply being a Taker. In the second option, you're repeating what your friend, colleague, or client has already told you about the great work you've done. It only makes sense that you help his or her friends, vendors, and clients with their legal needs; after all, if you knew a great doctor and your loved one was sick, wouldn't you want this doctor involved? The third option is great for the attorney who's afraid of using one of the other two techniques. In it, you're being honest in admitting that you're uncomfortable with asking, but are pushing yourself. By expressing your true feelings to your friend, colleague, or client, he or she will want to help you. That's what good people do for others.

Whichever option you choose, be sure to do this on the phone ahead of the meeting. There's a good chance your client will actually think up a few names before meeting with you. How nice would that be?

Tip #2: When meeting with a friend or relative, there are two important elements to focus on. The first is to be very curious. For example, if you're meeting with someone with whom you've not discussed much business, you could say, "I saw your profile on LinkedIn and am very interested in learning more about what you do. Really fascinating stuff." This sets up the opportunity to ask lots of questions, which can lead to openings for you to uncover business or legal problems. People love to talk about themselves, and asking questions helps you learn more about their professional needs.

The second element is asking for advice. Just as people love talking about themselves, they also love to give advice and opinions. You could say, "You're the best salesperson I've ever met. I'm looking to continue growing my practice, and I'd love to get your advice on the subject. Would you be open to discussing this when we meet on Thursday?"

Whichever direction you choose, little can be lost by asking questions or for advice. Typically, both of these approaches will lead to developing the relationship further and learning more about the opportunity in front of you.

As long as asking friends, colleagues, and clients for quality introductions is done in a nonaggressive manner, you'll be happy with the results. If this still seems hard for you, ask yourself these two questions: First, is obtaining an introduction from a friend or client easier or more difficult than from a stranger whom you've just met at a networking event? Second, what do you really have to lose? If the friend or client isn't open to making an introduction, then so be it. At least now you know where you stand with that individual, which is a good thing to know. (13-A)

F-E-A-R is False Evidence Appearing Real

What can you do to reduce your FEAR?

- Be prepared! Use scripts or an outline to set up introductions in a "sales-free" manner.
- Alter my scripts to make them more comfortable for you and how you speak.
- Create a list of friends and family and rate them A, B and C based on relationship and opportunity to help you.
- Start asking your best contacts for quality introductions first. Reach out to the contacts that are most likely to help you.
- Use the Quid Pro Quo method to help others first. This takes all the pressure off.
- Try to have 2-3 positive experiences right away. This will demonstrate to you how easy and beneficial asking can be.
- Become a master at asking for quality introductions and watch your book of business grow with less time invested in marketing.

13-A

CHAPTER THIRTEEN TAKEAWAYS

- Leveraging clients, colleagues, and friends makes a lot of sense. While attending events and conferences can be fruitful, nothing gets results like leveraging the people who already know and like you.
- Ask for a quality introduction prior to the face-to-face meeting using the "quid pro quo," "you're happy . . . should someone else be happy?," or "I'm not comfortable, but . . ." approach.
- Focus on asking questions and for advice to better understand your friends', colleagues', and clients' business issues, personal goals, and best relationships.

Network Note

"Since the advent of the smartphone, there has been no better tool for networking than LinkedIn. Not using LinkedIn is like throwing your smartphone in the toilet and going back to a rotary dial phone with a 6-foot chord."

—STEVE FRETZIN, AUTHOR

14

A Smarter Way to Use Social Media to Build Your Personal Brand and Drive New Business Development

While there are plenty of books written about social media, I've found that most attorneys have little time to invest in such trivial pursuits. I'm sure you've rolled your eyes a few times when perusing Facebook or Twitter and reading some of the material on those sites. Many of these negative opinions stem from reality, whereas others come from a disappointing lack of knowledge as to the sites' benefits.

In order to effectively utilize social media, it's important to recognize what you want social media to do for you. Are you looking to grow originations, develop a cult-like following, or brand yourself to get speaking engagements? By answering this question first, you can focus on investing your time in the most effective social media forums.

There are literally hundreds of social media channels to choose from. Being selective and focused on the right one will help you get results more quickly. For most attorneys, developing your brand in the business community is most important. In addition, you're most likely to get results from a social media channel that allows you to be proactive in developing new contacts and ultimately new business. In my experience, the best and fastest way to get results using social media is through LinkedIn.

Over the past ten years, LinkedIn has become the number one resource for helping brand and generate new business for service-based professionals. In many ways, it's better than Google because it's a business-networking platform rather than a general search platform. The ability to search and target people and organizations is unlimited.

LinkedIn is a fantastic brand-building tool that allows you to literally post your resume online. LinkedIn also helps you leverage your best contacts to make inside connections. Done properly, this can create a massive universe of followers, possible connections, and, most importantly, a cast of personal advocates willing to make quality introductions on your behalf.

Imagine being able to look at your client's list of friends, vendors, and associates prior to asking for a referral. You can search through LinkedIn's 50 million users to find the best inside connections for you.

Three Keys to Effectively Using LinkedIn

While there are hundreds of different tools on LinkedIn, here I want to give you the top three keys to effectively using LinkedIn. After reading this chapter, it's imperative that you invest a few hours exploring the site and practicing what you've learned. You should also try out some of the other features that aren't mentioned in this chapter. Finally, understand that LinkedIn is always evolving and changing, so the things you read in this chapter may not be 100-percent accurate six months from now. If you like what you read and how LinkedIn works for you, it's your responsibility to keep up to date on what's new and beneficial to you.

It might be helpful to look at LinkedIn while reading this chapter. You can use this chapter as a guide through the set-up process.

The first key to effectively using LinkedIn is to create a complete profile that best represents your expertise and experience in your field of practice. The second key is to develop your LinkedIn universe by adding the right contacts. The third key is to leverage those contacts and turn them into quality introductions. These three keys should initially take only a few hours to implement, and then as little as an hour a week to start producing results.

The First Key: Writing a LinkedIn Profile That Represents You Beautifully

In order to be effective on LinkedIn, you must have a professionally written and completed profile. Think of your LinkedIn page as your online resume and personal website. If the information online is incorrect, incomplete, or poorly written, it might stop someone from reaching out to you.

Imagine you're looking online for a remodeler for your home. The first site that comes up on Google looks fantastic. You click through to see some of the remodeling work the company has done, and the site says, "Sorry, cannot open this page." So you try another one. The same message comes up. If you're like me, you're done at that point. You just move on to the next search result. This is exactly what happens on LinkedIn without a skillfully written and finished profile.

Here are five tips to ensure your LinkedIn profile makes you look your best to potential clients and strategic partners:

Tip #1: Use a recent professional photograph on your LinkedIn page.

Most people are visual and want to see who they're going to be speaking with. As important as content is on a website, you've never seen one without images to back it up. Use the photo from your website if it's good, or get a headshot taken right away. It's not hard to do, but it can make all the difference when someone is checking out your profile. This may seem obvious, but don't post a cutesy picture with your kids, pet, or Halloween costume.

Tip #2: Have a professionally written background/summary.

Since your LinkedIn profile will be someone's first impression of you, failure to capture the reader's attention can move the reader quickly away. Personally, I like to see a summary written in the third person. It has the appearance of someone else boasting about your successes and best qualities without seeming egotistical.

If possible, keep your profile to three solid paragraphs. I enjoy reading profiles that read a little like a story. The first paragraph pulls you in. The second gets you familiar with the character. The third wraps things up and motivates you to take action.

Here's my LinkedIn profile as an example. It shares some personal information while also positioning my expertise as it relates to working with attorneys.

Driven, focused and passionate about helping attorneys to reach their full potential, Steve Fretzin is regarded as the premier business coach, speaker and author on business development for attorneys.

Over the past 12 years, Steve Fretzin has devoted his career to helping lawyers master the art of business development to achieve financial and personal freedom. His first book, "Sales-Free Selling," and more recently IICLE published book, "The Attorney's Networking Handbook," have changed the way attorneys look at business development forever.

Steve has been featured in the Chicago Tribune, Crain's and Entrepreneur.com. He has appeared on NBC News and WGN Radio, and has written articles for Attorney at Law magazine, the American Bar Association and the Illinois State Bar Association. You can also find his monthly column in the Chicago Daily Law Bulletin.

Please feel free to email or call Steve directly if you have any questions about business development or marketing your law practice.

Tip #3: Develop a strong list of skills that best represents your expertise.

If you take a few minutes and search some of your colleagues and competitors, you can quickly begin to formulate such a list. For example, an estate planning attorney would want to have the words "wills," "trusts," and "estate planning" listed among his or her skills, thus enabling people searching for an estate planner to more easily find the attorney.

Once your skills are posted, people in your network will then have the ability to endorse you. Essentially, when you have a skill that someone agrees with, they'll endorse you for that skill. While this might seem like "fluff," it's an important factor that people use to determine who are experts and who aren't. For example, if you had to choose between two referred doctors, one who has hundreds of positive endorsements on LinkedIn and one who has none, which would you choose? While this might seem insignificant, in the competitive legal environment everything counts.

Tip #4: Share your past business experience and education.

People like to know where you come from and where you've been. By providing an accounting of your past, people can see your track record of success and possible commonalities. For example, my background includes my experiences in the franchise area. For years, I not only sold franchises but also helped to support and develop them. This information has led to a number of great conversations with prospective clients about small businesses and how to run one effectively.

Remember, people like to do business with people they trust, and trust develops more easily when they've found a natural affinity. The more information you provide, the greater chance there is of connecting with someone. It's also important to list your college or law school as an easy way to start new business conversations with others from those same schools.

Tip #5: Customize your LinkedIn URL to better label your personal LinkedIn page.

You want your LinkedIn profile to have your name laid out for users. For example, an uncustomized name link looks like this:

www.linkedin.com/pub/john-smith/50/251/97

An editing feature in LinkedIn allows you to update your profile name so that it looks like this:

www.linkedin.com/in/johnsmith

As you can see, the second example is cleaner and will come up when people google "John Smith." This quick and simple edit will help to get you found and branded more effortlessly.

The Second Key: Strengthening Your Circle by Establishing the Very Best Connections

The second key to effectively using LinkedIn is to have the right strategy for your practice as it relates to adding connections.

As you may have observed, some people have fewer, less than 100 connections on LinkedIn while others have more than 10,000. How does this vast difference in number of connections affect the user's experience? How many connections should we have?

The answer is . . . it really depends. Ask yourself the following questions:

- "Do I want to use LinkedIn to brand myself as an expert, connect with existing relationships, or begin new relationships?"
- "Do I want to network with only my best relationships or with everyone?"
- "How much time can I really invest in working at LinkedIn?"
- "Am I targeting a niche where connectivity would be important?"

For example, if a managing partner of a firm never wants to be contacted by anyone for any reason, his or her number of connections on LinkedIn should be very low. In fact, he or she might want to consider not being on LinkedIn at all. On the other extreme, a legal recruiter would be looking to amass a huge network in order to have greater connectivity to the legal community and candidates for open positions.

Whether you decide on building a huge following or an intentionally small one, it's important for you to develop the right strategy for you! Here are three possible strategies to follow:

A "tight" strategy: Keep your connections limited to only your best and most trusted friends and clients. The idea here is that you only want or need to leverage 100 – 200 people to get the highest-level introductions. This is perfect for people who want more privacy, but still want to have connectivity with their best relationships. Managing partners or high-level partners who have strong networks and a limited amount of time for LinkedIn would use this strategy.

An "open" strategy: Be more open about who you connect with. Reach out and invite almost everyone in your database. You never know where business may come from next. Also, don't accept an invitation from someone you don't know. Focus on people with whom you've met or spoken and continue to grow your network.

An "all in" strategy: LinkedIn actually has an acronym for folks who follow this strategy. They're called LIONs, which stands for "LinkedIn open networkers." LIONs have over 10,000 1st-degree connections and are using LinkedIn as their primary source of prospecting for new business. They'll connect with anyone and accept all invitations to connect. This "all in" strategy is useful when you're looking to build a cult-like following or have almost limitless access to 2nd-degree connections. An example of a LION is a legal recruiter who's looking to find connections anywhere possible.

Whatever your strategy for adding connections, it's important to choose one before getting too far into the mix. You wouldn't want to invite thousands of people to connect with you and then change your mind and go small. While it's possible to remove people from your LinkedIn connections, it's not something you'd want to do thousands of times.

Another recommendation is to question solicitous invitations to connect. Be sure to review all invitations carefully before accepting or ignoring them. There are some people who want to connect to everyone regardless of who they are. Those people should be ignored if you're using a "tight" or "open" strategy since there may be limited value to you in connecting with them. On the other hand, others might want to connect because they're interested in you and what you do. It helps when someone writes you a personal message explaining why they want to connect. Take a moment to review an individual's profile before accepting or ignoring an invitation. You may discover a number of shared connections or things you have in common.

Once you've determined that you want to grow your LinkedIn connections, be sure to use the tools LinkedIn provides to its users. The system will allow you to select and search through Gmail, Outlook, Yahoo!, AOL, and IMAP to find a mass of names and e-mails of people you can invite to connect with you via LinkedIn. Using this feature is terrific because you won't have to invite people one at a time. The system will pull out e-mails from your databases, and then you can decide whom to include. I saw one of my clients go from 125 connections to over 500 just by using this feature, which took less than 30 minutes for him to accomplish.

Another nice feature is that you can customize a message to the group you're inviting to help them understand why you want to connect. This e-mail can be set up to look personalized to each individual, so they think you're e-mailing them alone, while in reality you're e-mailing everyone at once. This saves a lot of time!

Examples of a good customized message are

Dear _____,

I'm finally getting into the groove with LinkedIn and thought we could connect here. Please accept my invitation, and I hope we can help connect one another soon. Thanks!

or

Dear _____,

I'm using LinkedIn to stay in touch with my network and thought you might be open to connecting. Thanks, and I hope this finds you well.

This is much better than the traditional LinkedIn introduction that says, "I'd like to add you to my professional network on LinkedIn." Using a personalized message is more likely to result in someone connecting with you or checking out your profile.

The Third Key: Going Beyond Connecting and Turning LinkedIn Relationships into Better Introductions

The third key to effectively using LinkedIn is to be proactive in getting quality introductions. Before discussing that further, it's important to understand the basics of LinkedIn connectivity.

145

Within LinkedIn, there are three levels of connectivity. Your 1st-degree connections are the people you know. They're the ones who accepted your invitation to connect and you theirs.

Your 2nd-degree connections are the people your 1st-degree connections know and are connected with on LinkedIn. For example, Bob Jones is a connection of mine. I see on LinkedIn that he knows a man named Scott Williams. Therefore, Scott would be a 2nd-degree connection to me. If I know Bob and Bob knows Scott, would Bob make a quality introduction to Scott on my behalf? That's the million-dollar question.

Finally, there are the 3rd-degree connections — that would be Bob, speaking to Scott, speaking to Lou. Lou is three people away from me, which makes getting a quality introduction very difficult. My recommendation is to try to develop your network using your 2nd-degree connections.

Now let's target a close friend, client, or strategic partner to help us meet some new prospects. Essentially, you want to select one 1st-degree connection from your contact list in LinkedIn and pull him or her up on your screen.

If I'm looking at John Smith's profile, it might say 327 connections. Not only will it give you their names and titles, but it will show you whether they're 1st- or 2nd-degree connections. Focus on the 2nd-degree connections, as they're the folks you might be interested in meeting. If they were 1st degrees, you'd already know them.

Once you've pulled up John's contacts, you can quickly scan through his 327 names to find the people you'd like to meet. Make a list of the names that make the most sense for you, so that you can email or call John to discuss. If you're not comfortable with that, then have lunch together and inquire face-to-face. It's not considered stalking or spying to observe a possible connection with someone on LinkedIn; after all, when someone chooses to connect with you, they know that you're able to see each other's connections. Be polite and considerate when asking for the introduction, and <u>be sure to offer to make introductions for John as well</u>.

Another amazing way to proactively find connections on LinkedIn is through the "Search" feature located at the top left of the screen. You can easily use this feature to look up companies, industries or titles of people you may have interest in meeting.

For example, if I search for "general counsel" it pulls up over 76,000 results. Then I use the filters on the right of the screen to narrow down that list. Now I click on 2nd degree connections and GC's in the Greater Chicago area, which knocks the number down to 1,600. One more addition and I'll have my list. I will now click the "insurance" industry and my search is down to 37. Again, these are my 2nd degree connections with the title "General Counsel," in "Chicago" and in the "Insurance" industry.

Once I've used the search tool to identify the 37 GCs, I can review each person's profile individually to see WHOM we have in common. Under each GC's name and title, it lists out between 3-42 shared connections. Remember, these are the people that I know, that also may know these GC's.

The next step is the most important. You must "right click" the name of the GC and pull his name up in a separate tab. Once his or her profile is pulled up, click the "Mutual Connections" on the page. This will open up a box, which lays out the shared connections for you to review. Review the names and think about two things: first, your relationship to the shared connection (friend or acquaintance). Second, the possible connection your shared connection may have to the target (friend or acquaintance). You have more control with the stronger relationships, so you may want to isolate them first. Then, it makes sense to reach out to your connection and see if he is open to making a quality introduction. If he doesn't know the contact well enough, I may want to speak with another shared connection or decide to move on to another target. One way or another, I'll figure out whether there's a connection. I can then move forward to develop a new relationship or move on to the next person.

Based on your number of connections and the quality of the network you've assembled, you can be successful at using LinkedIn. The important thing is that you take a little time to investigate the site and the Search" feature to better understand how it works for you.

CHAPTER FOURTEEN TAKEAWAYS

- For 95 percent of lawyers, LinkedIn is the best social media tool to use. While all social media platforms may help in building one's brand, only LinkedIn is specifically designed for business professionals.

- The three keys to effectively using LinkedIn are (1) setting up a professional-looking profile, (2) adding connections based on an intelligent strategy that makes sense for you, and (3) using the "Advanced Search" feature to find the best 2nd-degree connections for you.
- LinkedIn is valuable to you as a business development tool only if you use it. As with most aspects of business development, you need to have a routine to get results. Just being on LinkedIn isn't going to add any real value to you or your practice.

Network Note

"It's crucial to leverage LinkedIn to build your network and stay engaged with the community, add value to your connections, and strategically open doors for potential opportunities."

—TRICIA MEYER, MEYER LAW, LTD.

Conclusion: Now It's Time to Execute!

So, what have you learned? More importantly, what will you execute on to improve your chances of success as at networking?

As a general philosophy, I created, use, and teach the "3 Ps" methodology of success. If you look at any professional athlete, classical musician, or top chef, you'll observe that they had to follow plans and leverage processes to improve their performance and become the best at their craft. The 3 Ps methodology does exactly this.

Let's review them so that you can better understand how to use what you've learned.

The first P stands for "Planning."

As you now know, without a roadmap to follow, you're merely guessing at where and how you should spend your business development time.

The second P is "Process."

This could be how you create your infomercial or how you meet someone for a networking one-on-one meeting. Without processes to follow, you're just out there "winging it" and hoping for a positive outcome. In my experience, this is rarely a good way to invest your time.

The last P is "Performance Improvement."

This means that you'll need to try out your new plan and processes when networking and then give yourself honest feedback about how you did and how effective you were.

A good analogy is to imagine a quarterback who routinely gets sacked throughout the game. The coach and the quarterback must make changes to the game plan in order to stop the sacking. Processes are only as good as the person executing them. Failure is not the bad guy; one's inability to learn from failure is! Do whatever it takes to improve through the experiences created.

Don't be afraid to change things or adapt them to your personality. You must take ownership of these new processes to enjoy leveraging the new skills covered in this book. That being said, don't change them so much that they lose their effectiveness in helping you to develop new business.

As you can imagine, it takes a lot of confidence and hard work to become a great networker. Even with my advice, you still need to take the reins and make good things happen. If it helps, start small. Don't feel that you have to attend five events a month or meet with ten new people right away. Depending on your current skill level with networking, it's okay to start slow and work your way up.

A great way to improve performance is to debrief your networking meetings directly after they happen, which will help you uncover mistakes and skipped steps. Only by realizing our missteps can we improve and not repeat them. Here are Fretzin's top 10 questions to ask yourself after meeting with someone new:

NETWORKING DEBRIEFING QUESTIONS

1. "Did I research my prospective strategic partner prior to meeting with him or her?"
2. "Did I use that research to build rapport and find natural affinities?"

3. "Did I use all of the steps in setting a clear agenda for our meeting?"
4. "Did I ask pertinent questions to learn more about my strategic partner's background, business goals, and best leads?"
5. "Did I use my infomercial to gain understanding and buy-in from the strategic partner?"
6. "Did I use stories/examples to describe how I help people and explained who is a good lead for me?"
7. "Did I use T-L-E-N-D (see Chapter 11) to better understand if the strategic partner is qualified to invest more time with?"
8. "If the person is qualified to be a strategic partner, did I end the meeting with one introduction being offered to each other?
9. "Did I obtain a name and coach my strategic partner to make a quality introduction?"
10. "Did I establish a specific next step to ensure both parties are committed to seeing this new relationship flourish?"

At the end of the day, the goal is efficiency. This means quality over quantity. It might be better to attend one high-level event and meet three solid prospects than attend three events and meet nine unqualified people. Your time invested would be cut by 66 percent, and you'd get better results as well.

My greatest hope is that you'll use the tools presented in this book to work less and make more. After all, as everyone knows, time is money.

Bonus Chapter: Networking Stories from the Vault

I thought it might be fun to ask some of the best networkers I know to share some of their funny, crazy, or heartwarming networking stories. These stories all have a point or moral. In some cases, the moral is to run away as fast as you can from the Takers you meet. Another is to hang in there for the pot of gold at the end of the rainbow. I hope you enjoy these stories and draw a few takeaways to help you in your networking endeavors.

Here's one of mine:

"Remember how I told you that you could learn from my mistakes? Here's one of them: I've been burned in the past by trying to help people before really knowing what they were all about.

Let me tell you a quick story to explain.

In my first year of networking, I didn't just refer business. I became a referral machine. I was referring people that I met at will. From a karma point of view, I was absolutely glowing.

However, one day I met a lactation consultant at a local chamber of commerce event. They say timing is everything. My sister had just delivered her son and for some reason she had shared with me that her baby wasn't catching on. Well, I put two and two together and immediately made the introduction. Everyone seemed happy with my bighearted gesture.

Great, right? Well, maybe not so great.

A few days later I received a call from my sister, and she was in tears. She'd met with this lactation consultant, and it was an absolute disaster! She told my sister that if she decided not to breastfeed her baby, she'd be killing her child.

I had no idea from meeting this lady briefly at the local event that she was, in effect, a "lactation zealot."

The moral of this story is to be really careful about whom you refer. I know now that if I'd taken the time to meet with this lady first, I never would have referred her to my sister.

This ended up being a bad news, good news situation in the end. The bad news was that my sister had a horrible experience, and the good news was that I learned a valuable lesson in networking effectively."

Steve Fretzin, Author

*   *   *

"Broadly speaking, networking requires relationships and relevance. The two stories set forth below are contextual examples of these basic and immutable principles.

Part of my plan as a business developer was to be a "go to" lawyer for overseas investments in the U.S. We joined and then built an international law group. Two networking stories emerge. Both involve conversations in a different type of "bar" at 2:00 in the morning. The first occurred in a bar in Amsterdam and involved building a relationship through the evening with a lawyer from the U.S. At the end of the evening after discussing our firms and approaches, I said to him, "Oh, did I mention that we also have good litigators?" The next morning, he referred me to a friend of his who had some litigation in Chicago and was displeased with his existing lawyer. That client turned out to be a very good source for litigation as well as transactional work. Fortunately, I hadn't just relied on the "relationship" without demonstrating "relevance" (i.e., the presence of litigation expertise), or this client would likely not have materialized.

A second 2:00 a.m. bar story occurred in Bologna. An Israeli lawyer and I were discussing venture capital investments in each other's countries. I asked him to consider my forming a group of Americans to fly to Israel and meet his clients and see if there were mutual opportunities. This turned into three successful business trips to Israel and the establishment of many strong relationships with his (and now our) clients. If I had just relied on my relationship and not shown relevance to him, this opportunity would not have arisen."

Fred Tannenbaum, Managing Partner, Gould & Ratner LLP

*   *   *

"Networking is one of the easiest and hardest methods to obtain business. Most people think that

it's just about handing out your business cards and telling your story. That method draws little business and bores prospective clients. When you follow up with them, you are usually ignored because they view you as a 'sales person,' and nobody likes to be 'sold.'

Early in my sales career, I was told to join a multi-township chamber of commerce. There were always hundreds of people at these meetings, and it seemed to be nothing more than a big social club. My manager told me to be myself and not to sell our services at these meetings. Then he sent me off alone to my first meeting. As a rookie salesperson, I didn't really know what to say to these strangers. I just stood by little clusters of three to five people and listened in on their conversations. After a while, I noticed they all talked like long-time friends, and there was very little 'shop talk.'

It was at this first event that I discovered a technique that I would end up using the rest of my career while networking. The key was to concentrate on the other person and ask questions about them and their services. 'How long have you been with ABC Company? How did you get started with that? What tips would you suggest for networking with the chamber? How long have you been a member? Did you receive any new business from the chamber?' Then I asked one more question: 'What did you do before your current position with ABC Company?'

It sounds simple, but by asking good questions, people think you are a great conversationalist. They like you more and want to help you. For me, I was amazed that the people I met would walk me around and introduce me to actual prospects!

I found the secret. If people get to know and like you, they will want to help you. So don't tell your "story" or pitch, but rather ask them about their life. That is the key to developing new relationships and eventually new business."

Bill Clayton, Financial Consultant AR
Specialist, TransWorld Systems, Inc.

* * *

"There is nothing like connecting personally with your clients to cement your relationship. Whether attending a wedding, children's milestones, or memorials for deceased relatives, when you work closely with someone, you can become like family.

For those clients with children, one way to connect is through their kids. It just so happened that as some of our clients were having children, my college age daughter was looking for babysitting jobs. So in addition to paying us for legal work, some clients started paying her to babysit. Of course, this could have gone terribly wrong, as there is nothing worse than upsetting someone about their children. This could really sour a good client relationship. Fortunately, I had confidence in my daughter's babysitting skills and manner. In the end, it created a fun and supportive client connection."

Douglas Masters, Managing Partner,
Chicago Office, Loeb & Loeb LLP

*   *   *

"I became the president of Chicago SHRM (Society for Human Resource Management) because my friend Sally was the president before me. I met Sally at a volunteer committee meeting ten years prior to that. She selected me as her VP because I introduced her to one of my clients who hired her. My client sold his business, but the new owner saw the value of Sally's contribution, and she was promoted to a bigger job with more responsibility. There was a change of control in that company two more times. The final change involved the company being bought by Google. Today, Sally heads up the 'Learning and Development' department for the Americas. She flies all around the world training Googlers.

Sally also has three children. One time, she was speaking with another parent at a school event who happened to mention he had a need for an HR consultant. Sally quickly recommended me to this parent. I now have a new client and a four-month project has grown into an open-ended engagement. I am helping them to develop their HR strategy and find a VP of HR. I am now networking with other colleagues within Chicago SHRM to identify talent to fill that role.

Try joining an association that is relevant to your business or practice. Be an active contributor and work to develop long-term relationships. Connections are everywhere!"

Carol Semrad, C. Semrad & Associates

*   *   *

"I have been networking for a long, long time now. I am a business and life coach who helps people to bring out their best self. I have been networking for many years and have met people I liked and people I really didn't like, people who could refer business and individuals who were just not a good fit for me.

About six years ago, I walked into a networking event quite far from my neighborhood. This was about nine or ten years into my business networking experience. I was introduced to a woman and something quite spectacular happened. I felt a physical jolt. I sensed something that felt dynamic and exciting. The voice within me said, 'I need to know this person!'

I was told that she was also a coach, but I believed she coached something different than I did. It took a couple of months, but she is now someone who has referred many clients to me and someone to whom I have referred many clients and people of influence. She is someone from whom I continue to learn general lessons and specific business tips. She has become not only a best friend but also part of my family. We are now coauthors of an upcoming book on business, sales, and speaking.

Networking can be physically and mentally draining sometimes; however, I have found great treasures from the relationships that have been developed. By investing time with the right people, I have developed a successful coaching business and established some amazing personal relationships."

Linda McCabe, Optimal Level LLC

Made in the USA
Lexington, KY
09 November 2019

56607268R00098